SECRETS OF THE
HARD SELL

SECRETS OF THE HARD SELL

N. C. Christensen

PARKER PUBLISHING COMPANY, INC.

WEST NYACK, NEW YORK

© 1975 *by*

Parker Publishing Company, Inc.
West Nyack, New York

Library of Congress Cataloging in Publication Data

Christensen, N   C
  Secrets of the hard sell.

  1. Salesmen and salesmanship. I. Title.
HF5438.C544136   658.85   74-28190
ISBN 0-13-798058-2

Printed in the United States of America

A Book About You
to Put Your Success Program
in High Gear

This book charts the way for you to jack up your sales by 10 percent, or 15 percent, or 50 percent, and that's only the beginning. The limit of your potential is still ahead of you. *Secrets of the Hard Sell* may even double your volume. It can do the same with your personal income. This book charts a course whereby you can realize your most ambitious dreams.

This book was written about *you* and for *you!*

This book was written by a salesman to benefit other salesmen.

This book is targeted in on three objectives vital to *you!* . . . Check these three objectives now:

OBJECTIVE NO. 1.—To provide an arsenal of HARD SELL SECRETS with which to speed up your success in selling. These principles can make selling easier for you. They can make selling more profitable for you. More thrilling. More satisfying.

OBJECTIVE NO. 2.—To present HARD SELL in its true light. THE HARD SELL in this light is no bombastic method of peddling. THE HARD SELL has been eliminated from the "buyer beware" category. THE HARD SELL, as presented to you here refers to a refined, persuasive, highly ethical, status-building form of selling. THE HARD SELL exudes a magic power which can enrich your bank account. It provides an exciting approach to a higher status for you in selling.

OBJECTIVE NO. 3—To show *you* how others have mastered the *Secrets of the Hard Sell,* and have profited by them, and to show you how to harness the magic power of THE HARD SELL.

This book teaches you how to turn the *Secrets of the Hard Sell* into cash assets for you. You get hard-hitting, practical principles in work-a-day language.

From this book *you* learn how to develop dynamic power for your sales presentations.

In this book you are shown how to make each selling hour pay off better for you.

Check these vital chapter references now:

Chapter 1 discloses the No. 1 SECRET OF THE HARD SELL.

Chapter 2 hooks a big dollar mark to prospecting with the dynamic thrust of *Secrets of the Hard Sell.*

Chapter 4 is a problem solver for you. This is priceless for you when you slip into a selling rut. It gives you fresh views of the come-back power in cold-call selling.

Chapter 5 tells you about the magic selling power in words. It tells you how to make your sales presentations live. It tells you what to do to create a desire to buy.

Chapter 7 contains prescriptions for mellowing the most stubborn prospects.

Chapter 11 deals with insults. You do encounter them now and then in selling. This chapter suggests ways of handling those situations. It tells you how to convert insults into sales.

Principles presented in this book have withstood test after test in competitive market situations. They have proved to be sales builders. Each chapter is loaded with motivating, usable selling power. Guidelines are provided to lead you into the abundant pastures of super-salesmanship.

How to convert *Secrets of the Hard Sell* into immediate sales gains is made clear. It's all here—the stimulating story of the magic power discovered in the *Secrets of the Hard Sell.* To profit by it read on. Then release the power of *Secrets of the Hard Sell* principles in your drive for a greater share of the business available.

To you and to all others who recognize that persuasive salesmanship is the actual payroll builder in industry, this book is dedicated.

N.C.C.

OTHER BOOKS BY THE AUTHOR

The Art of Persuasion in Selling   1970

The Art of Persuasion for Sales Managers   1971

The Magic Power of Command Selling   1973

CONTENTS

12. Regaining Lost Business Through Hard Sell Magic (*continued*)

1

How the Hard Sell Builds
Volume and Personal Income

Believe it! The HARD SELL is loaded with magic power. Today's HARD SELL has been refined, stripped clean of the ancient notion that HARD SELL meant some sort of deception. From that ancient notion sprang the warning: "Buyer beware." . . . Now the refined *Secrets of the Hard Sell* embody such virtues as these:

- Convincing, provable facts are glorified.
- More captivating demonstrations reveal more facts and more benefits.
- More vivid demonstrations are based on honesty.
- More persistent follow-through, with a steady flow of facts, provide HARD SELL continuity.
- More HARD SELL persuasion to carry buyers to a satisfying decision.

Optimism is a major element in the HARD SELL. Take your own case for instance. You have experienced the invigorating effect of landing a hard-to-close sale. Wasn't it sound optimism, plus enthusiasm that got the business for you? Optimism and enthusiasm knock down sales barriers every day for those who go after business with honest intent and HARD SELL vigor.

A salesman I know mastered the *Secrets of the Hard Sell* and soared from an "average" salesman's berth to a super-salesman's perch.

That salesman became trusted as a marketing specialist.

His advice was sought by buyers, prospective buyers, and by his colleagues, who wanted to know the secret of his HARD SELL SUCCESS.

Each upward step he took was based on principles of the HARD SELL. One of the secrets of his success was this: "At the end of each day I evaluate what I have done. I seek opportunities I may have overlooked. I am restless about achieving total coverage."

Another high-production, HARD SELL salesman challenged a group of us one morning. He asked: "Why don't you beef up your sales pitches? Why don't you give your prospects the HARD SELL treatment?" To those queries, we added these six steps to the "beef up" ladder of success:

1. RAISE YOUR SIGHTS. Look up, up and up. See those new heights of opportunity up there? Reach for them. Tackle them.

2. BE STATUS-MINDED. See yourself as a super-salesman.

3. DIG DEEPER. Search for new ways to serve. Master the *Secrets of the Hard Sell.*

4. INNOVATE. Be an idea man. Exploit the magic power that you'll discover in the *Secrets of the Hard Sell.*

5. BE CONVINCING. Show your prospects how they can benefit by buying from you. Prove your point.

6. FOLLOW THROUGH. Hang on! Every prospect is a live one until he's sold. Then he requires regular re-suscitation. The HARD SELL FOLLOW THROUGH pays off in the *long run.*

Repeated calls have HARD SELL POWER. You may just drop in to make sure that your customer's last order came through in good shape. That's HARD SELL in a velvet glove. Your sincere interest impresses your customers. This HARD SELL SECRET has two-fisted selling power.

The No. 1 SECRET OF THE HARD SELL is quite simple. This is it:

RESTLESS CREATIVITY.

This simple secret builds sales volume. Doing this builds *you* up. It also builds up your personal income.

Let us now consider the selling power in a much-used two-letter word. The word is *IF*. Take another look at that word. Ponder it. Notice how restless that word is? Let us assume that you are presenting your product or service to a prospect. You suggest to him: "There can be a lot of new, profitable business for you in this . . . *IF* . . ." Immediately you are off on a creative HARD SELL presentation.

Now try the *IF* on yourself:

There can be more business for you *IF* you innovate.

You can increase your HARD SELL power *IF* you think it through.

You can add magic sales power to your demonstrations *IF* you activate your creative ability and release its full selling power.

The record proves that RESTLESS CREATIVITY is loaded with the magic power of the HARD SELL. This places it in the No. 1 spot of *Secrets of the Hard Sell.* In case after case, RESTLESS CREATIVITY has increased sales volume and personal incomes.

How the Hard Sell Can Up Your Pay Check 100 Percent

Now that we know why RESTLESS CREATIVITY is the No. 1 SECRET OF THE HARD SELL let's explore the possibilities in CREATIVE RESTLESSNESS.

The No. 1 Secret we are examining here is a far cry from worry. You have met salesmen who worry themselves through the day. Yet, they come out with a fair return. You may also know of salesmen who plan their days in advance. You have noticed how methodical they are. You have also noticed that they are creative—restlessly creative. At will they summon an endless flow of fresh ideas. If you peek into the paymaster's books, you probably will discover that the pay checks of these restless, creative salesmen have more and larger figures on them than the checks made out for the worry bugs.

I worked with a salesman who firmly believed that the maximum effort in the HARD SELL should begin immediately after the first order is signed. "As soon as a sale is closed and I present a copy of the order to a customer I try to lay the groundwork right then for another order. Either I get another order then or I leave the door open for my early return. With one order in the bag I am on my way to developing that account into a heavier buying customer."

I observed the progress of that salesman for some time. I saw him step up his income 100 percent. I also saw him take off from that 100 percent launching pad, headed for a 200 percent increase. And he made it, and more. Here are some of the motivating requirements which that salesman placed upon himself:

(a) Crack a new account daily.

(b) Keep communication lines open to prospects and to customers.

(c) Don't fret. There's more business ahead if I go after it with the magic power in the HARD SELL.

(d) Follow through!

5-Point Success Plan With Hard Sell Thrust

I was lunching with another salesman in a town hit hard by an economic slump. "This town is going to come out on top," my companion remarked with wide-eyed optimism. "Why?" I asked. He replied: "Every prospect I have met today and yesterday has been eager to pry into any idea I presented. They want to get back to making money. Show them how and they'll buy," he snapped.

Brief examination on my part disclosed the secrets of this man's success. He had five HARD SELL points in his favor. He was:

1. CREATIVELY OPTIMISTIC. He sold the "hope" idea. He cut through gloom. He made it appear to be possible, desirable, even enticing.

2. CREATIVELY RESTLESS. That salesman's best

selling product was an idea on which his prospects could cash in.

3. CREATIVELY OBJECTIVE. He kept the spotlight on his prospects. He glamorized their dreams.

4. BOLD IN SALES PRESENTATIONS. He put excitement into his sales pitches. He generated a contagious fever for what he had to sell.

5. DEPENDABLY HONEST. He created confidence. He showed by his relationship with customers that he was a man of integrity. He also proved the integrity of his product. He profited by the magic of HARD SELL confidence in himself and what he sold. He spread an "I can do it" spirit in his associations.

Those five HARD SELL points kept that salesman's income on a steady climb. They were the keys to his success. Applying them to his operation, he scored high in sales and in sales gains. He had mastered the lucrative *Secrets of the Hard Sell*. He was inspired to put those secrets into action. Being restlessly creative he applied those HARD SELL principles to himself. He allowed his RESTLESS CREATIVITY to take over. This creative spirit was the seed of his HARD SELL power. He recognized this as *you* can.

Secret of Changing "Lost" Accounts into Eager Buyers

Your first step in changing the attitude of a "lost" account is to solve the mystery of the loss. This done, you face this immediate challenge: "How can I regain that lost business?"

In the No. 1 SECRET OF THE HARD SELL you will find your answer to that challenging question. RESTLESS CREATIVITY has discovered ways of altering attitudes from buying resistance to eagerness to buy. Let's examine three tested methods of changing "lost" accounts into active buyers:

1. MAINTAIN YOUR INTEREST IN THE WELFARE OF YOUR CUSTOMER. Go back to him

again and again. Pump new life into the account by HARD SELL PERSUASION. Keep your personal self-interest out of the picture. Concentrate on that "lost" customer.

2. TAKE YOUR "LOST" CUSTOMER INTO YOUR CONFIDENCE. Ask him for his opinion on a point vital to the sale. This act implies that you believe he is a man who knows. You have touched his ego. You have boosted his status. He begins to feel good toward you. This is the HARD SELL in a velvet glove.

3. GO IN LOADED. Go to your "lost" customer with an idea. Present something fresh, something solid, something that touches his self-interest. This pitch is for his personal benefit, not yours. Seek his advice. Get him into the act. If he attempts to freeze you out, don't freeze. Instead, keep talking about him. Speak warmly, smoothly about his business, about HIS possibilities for making money. Doing this you melt the ice. You drive in a wedge so the magic selling power of the HARD SELL can gain renewed admittance to the man and get in its licks.

Salesmen who forget a sale a few hours after they walk out with a first order risk loss of accounts. New accounts, like new plants in a garden, require nourishment. The restlessly creative salesman is constantly nourishing his accounts with the fertility of ideas. This is HARD SELL at its most productive best.

I once read a message on a man's desk that told me what sort of guy he was. That neatly framed message had a solid punch. It drove home to me this bit of simple HARD SELL gossip: *"Think It Through."*

The man behind that desk demonstrated that he has the ability to think it through. He boasted of his first victory in "rescuing" a "lost" customer. He recovered that account by the magic power of the HARD SELL. He hammered away on that "lost" customer until he made a believer out of him. This is how he did it: (a) He made his presentations very persuasive; (b) he was persistent; (c) he stepped into the other man's shoes so he could think the problem through from his prospect's point of view; (d) he remained RESTLESSLY CREATIVE as he exerted HARD SELL pressure on that "lost" account. Ultimately, he changed that man into a most eager buyer.

Another salesman demonstrated how to change a "lost" customer into an eager buyer also by HARD SELL power. A lukewarm manufacturing account challenged him. A flood of orders had dulled the thinking of the factory management. They cut back on product promotion. The advertising salesman tried to penetrate that armor of self-contentment. But, in time the inevitable happened. The factory began losing business. Government orders were cut back. The factory laid off part of its force. Myopic salesmen backed away from that account. The advertising salesmen thought it through. He found undeveloped sales possibilities for that factory and for himself. He had an idea. He prodded his home office into action to back him up. By RESTLESS CREATIVITY he exposed new market areas and new techniques for selling the products of the factory. He went to the factory management with a constructive promotion program. He had become an idea man. The factory management bought his idea. Results were good. Sales turned upward. That salesman had pulled his slipping account out of a slump. He received his personal reward in greater sales volume. This was his dividend for RESTLESS CREATIVITY in harness with the magic power of the HARD SELL.

Neglected accounts often become "lost" accounts. They have a way of freezing out a salesman. Frequent call-backs, with a HARD SELL purpose, have a warming effect if the salesman concentrates on the welfare of his customers. When you stop in to ask how the last shipment has been selling or how it arrived, the attention of your customer automatically turns to buying. This action combines good-will-building power with the HARD SELL. It opens the way to better serve the customer. That alone carries a HARD SELL wallop.

Another creatively restless salesman established a record of reviving old accounts and opening new ones by a simple method: he committed himself to making at least one call after quitting time. He aimed these extra calls at "lost" accounts. This called for discrimination in choosing his prospects. He made this suggestion: "Resist the temptation to break in on a prospect who is putting on his coat preparatory to leaving his office. But, on the other hand, *If* your prospect appears to be relaxed move in on him with a tempting idea."

An old-timer in supplying farmers and ranchers with batteries, tools, and other items was spotted one evening by an observing and restlessly creative salesman. The salesman approached him with a suggestion for boosting battery sales. In minutes he had the old timer considering new uses for batteries. The salesman pointed out the cumulative possibilities in volume-buying. The volume, of course, was that salesman's optimistic view of his proposal to promote battery sales. The old-timer became optimistic, too, and enthusiastic. The HARD SELL pitch of that restlessly creative salesman had taken effect. The end result was the development of a fat account from an unspectacular account.

Secret of Laying Down a Concentrated Hard Sell Barrage

We are now talking about militant selling in tough situations. This is a far cry from the milk-toast approach to make a sale. The HARD SELL BARRAGE WE ARE TALKING ABOUT is a hard-hitting drive for: (a) New business; (b) for increased sales to established accounts.

To make this sales offensive succeed we tie it in with the No. 1 SECRET OF THE HARD SELL. This requires imaginative planning. To develop the maximum power of a frontal attack for business we discipline ourselves to do these three things:

1. NIGHTTIME PLANNING. This conditions us for a HARD SELL ASSAULT in the morning.
2. DISCRIMINATING SELECTION OF PROSPECTS. This cuts down on fruitless effort. It sets up live objectives for our MORNING HARD SELL ASSAULTS.
3. DRAMATIZING IDEAS. This dresses up our ideas in the attractiveness of self-interest for our prospects. We aim straight at the "heart"—the pocketbook of potential buyers.

Before touching off your HARD SELL BARRAGE remind yourself that nighttime planning can be highly productive. It saves you from biting into your daylight time for selling.

Remind yourself also to enrich your plans with provable benefits for those who buy. Show them how others have profited

Evaluate each prospect for your early morning assault. Be realistic. Ask yourself these questions:

(a) Is this prospect financially qualified to buy more of my goods than he has been buying?

(b) Can he profit by buying more now? Why?

(c) Is my projected presentation based on the best interests of this prospective buyer?

(d) Are my ideas for this account based on well-researched knowledge of his capability to profit by what I have to sell?

(e) Am I sold on my own idea? Am I excited about it?

Ideas become alluring when they are linked with the No. 1 SECRET OF THE HARD SELL. If those ideas are the products of RESTLESS CREATIVITY, they will have depth and HARD SELL PERSUASIVE QUALITIES.

Now, reread the two questions on line "e" above. They relate to the nerve center of any sales barrage. Unless you are excited about the whole deal, your contemplated bombardment will turn out to be a dud. Any sale has two elements: *you* and your prospect. This puts the success of a CONCENTRATED HARD SELL BARRAGE squarely up to you. Unless you become excited over your own idea, it will fizzle out. On the other hand, *If* you get worked up about it, sales barriers will crumble. Combine a creative idea with an exciting, convincing presentation and you have the ingredients of the HARD SELL with its many SECRET POWERS.

Most masters of the HARD SELL have one thing in common. They concentrate their HARD SELL POWER to break down sales resistance. They seize attention with a HARD SELL BARRAGE. They generate interest in what they have to sell. They do this with HARD SELL DEMONSTRATION. They create desire for what they have to sell. They do this by drumming hard on benefits for their prospects. They maintain this HARD SELL TEMPO in their presentations. They close with a CONCENTRATED BARRAGE OF FACTS. In that way they get buying action through the magic power of the HARD SELL.

One master of the HARD SELL told me how he did it. He listed five keys to his success:

1. "I plan my work with one idea in mind—TO SELL! Then I work that plan to the limit.

2. "I respect my prospect's time. I never waste it. I'm also stingy with my own time. If I'm not headed in the direction of a sale I'm wasting time.

3. "I'm ahead of time on appointments. This gives me time to size up a situation.

4. "I build sales on courtesy, optimism and imagination.

5. "I exchange ideas with other salesmen. I've found that I have no monopoly on the good ideas."

The secret of laying down a HARD SELL BARRAGE is to: (a) Know your product. Know its quality. Know how to use it profitably. (b) Know your prospect. Know his needs. Know his desires. (c) Concentrate on benefiting your prospects. Keep them in the spotlight. Glorify benefits for them. (d) Spice your presentations with colorful facts (e) Dramatize your demonstrations. (f) Capitalize on the HARD SELL with humor and its magic power.

There is magic power in humor, but one word of caution: Never, but never, make your prospect the butt of any joke. Use yourself as the boob if there must be one. George Ade, a great humorist, appreciated the HARD SELL power in good humor. He once wrote:

"If you can only land your shot under a man's funny bone you have done the deadly work and can interest him in whatever you have to offer."

Hard Sell Secrets of Building Small Accounts into Fat, Profitable Accounts

Some of us in selling are criticized for working too hard and thinking too little. This gets us right down to the muscle in *Secrets of the Hard Sell*.

I recall one of the busiest salesmen I have ever known. He was the "go-go" type. He would swing out of traffic, park his car, trot away to tackle a prospect. Back in minutes, he would drive on to repeat the performance just a few blocks away. He had a large list of prospects. He had more than enough prospects on his call list for a constructive day's work. When darkness drove him out of the market place and into his home, he would tally results of his frantic day. He got business from most of his calls. However, a cold and critical look at the business he had written finally told him that he had been just taking orders. He wasn't really selling. He was writing up lots of small orders that the HARD SELL could have developed into fat, profitable accounts. This salesman made a decision: He would think in terms of bigger sales. This was sound thinking.

That salesman needed to put the No. 1 SECRET OF THE HARD SELL to work for him. RESTLESS CREATIVITY could direct his energy into richer channels. He tried thinking about how to sell more of his product to his small accounts. He later admitted to me that he had been thinking too little and earning too little. Instead of profiting by the *Secrets of the Hard Sell,* he had been snatching small orders on a hit-run basis.

One of the successful automobile salesmen on my list, Artie Fisk, was a RESTLESSLY CREATIVE man. He'd come up with a "hot" idea about how Mr. Reynolds could profit by using three cars instead of one in his business. Artie spent "idle" time finding out how Mr. Reynolds operated his business. He figured out the cost of time Mr. Reynolds wasted when his sub-executives had to wait to use the one car available. He broke down all this observation and research into dollar benefits which Mr. Reynolds could enjoy by buying additional executive transportation. This done, Artie turned on his most persuasive HARD SELL power. This changed that one-car user to a three-car user. That salesman with an idea also succeeded in keeping the door open at that place for additional future business. A once small account became a fat, profitable account. And because of that, Artie Fisk has become a welcomed idea man. Other accounts have sought him out and they, too, have profited, as he has.

How to Stick Your Neck Out
to Win Hard Sell Success

Various avenues are open to salesmen to swell small accounts into more profitable proportions. Grasshopper selling seldom ac-

complishes this. The HARD SELL requires RESTLESS CRE-
ATIVITY coupled with the magic of HARD SELL ACTION.
For instance:

> . . . A uniform salesman was stumped by the "no solici-
> tors" sign that suddenly showed up on many hospital and
> medical clinic doors. His restless, creative mind led him into
> "exclusive showings" of his line in rented rooms near to those
> hospitals. The idea paid off in profitable volume.

> . . . A printing salesman convinced a bank that personal
> calls by bank personnel to present greeting cards and cal-
> endars to desirable accounts would be profitable for the bank.
> It was. It was also profitable on a continuing basis for the
> salesman.

> . . . A wholesale furniture salesman persuaded a small
> buyer of his line to permit the salesman to display his varied
> line in window and floor space in the store. He served refresh-
> ments to his callers. He distributed literature on the quality
> line. He made HARD SELL contacts with influential people.
> Inquiries began coming to the store management. Sales in this
> quality line picked up. The dealer became impressed. He also
> became a larger buyer of the line. This, too, resulted from a
> salesman's RESTLESS CREATIVITY—the No. 1 SECRET
> OF THE HARD SELL.

> . . . A haberdashery salesman's business totaled consid-
> erably more than his colleagues' in the same house. He made
> his gains by a direct HARD SELL "vanity" appeal to well
> selected prospects. Each morning he made one or two calls
> to fashion-conscious prospects whom he had thoughtfully
> classified. He informed those prospects that he had one or two
> "special numbers" in a new shipment, that he had put those
> specials aside for those prospects to pass judgment on them.
> He thus pinned each prospect down for a fixed-time special
> private showing. This was HARD SELL in a velvet glove.
> No deception. Just hard facts. Definite commitments placed
> the prospects in the role of fashion experts. They also placed
> the prospects in a mood of anticipation, vulnerable for the
> magic power in the HARD SELL.

The HARD SELL secret of success in many cases is restlessness. And it is RESTLESS CREATIVITY we have defined as the

No. 1 SECRET OF THE HARD SELL. Even the inventive genius, Thomas A. Edison, recognized the potency of restlessness in progress. He said:

"Restlessness is discontent—and discontent is the first necessity of progress. Show me a thoroughly satisfied man . . . . and I will show you a failure."

In case after case, salesmen profit by sticking their neck out. They do this to put over an idea and they lean heavily on the magic power in the HARD SELL. James A. Conant, diplomat and educator, made this observation which can be significant in the HARD SELL:

"Behold the turtle. He makes progress only when he sticks his neck out."

2

Scoring a Million with the Secrets of Hard Sell Prospecting

Gene is a restless, creative salesman. He is optimistic. He works hard. The No. 1 SECRET OF THE HARD SELL stimulates him. It keeps his chin up.

You can do the same as Gene does and profit by it. You may be doing better than Gene. In either case, Gene has his sights high. He aims at scoring a million. "I fully intend to hit the million mark in sales," he assures us.

Gene's starting point was a natural. He began with HARD SELL PROSPECTING. He still prospects every day. He mixes prospecting with hard selling. He prospects on his way to lunch. He prospects while seated in his favorite cafe or club. Gene says: "There are prospects rubbing against me wherever I go. My big job is figuring out how my product can become beneficial to each of them. I'm never short on prospects. This gets down to a matter of qualifying them and classifying them. That is a pleasant nighttime activity for me. When my family quiets down and I sit alone with my thoughts, a pencil, and a pad of paper, I do my most constructive and productive prospecting."

You see, Gene understands the secret of scoring a million. He has a specific figure in mind to shoot at. He keeps firing away at that million dollar mark. That's his target. And, a similar opportunity is within your reach. For example, consider prospecting with the magic power in HARD SELL. The following ideas might be effective as opening shots for you:

1. WHAT IS A PROSPECT? The obvious answer is this: A prospect is a buyer of what you have to sell. How many of such have you passed up today?

2. THE LIVE PROSPECT? Adapt your product to the advantageous use of a selected individual. Now you have a "live" prospect.

3. MAKE YOUR PROSPECT LIST SELECTIVE. Give it "life." Include those who you have decided can use your product to their advantage. Now go after that individual. Call on the *Secrets of the Hard Sell* to put persuasive punch into your approach.

4. SEEK NEW SOURCES for prospective buyers. Search them out as you travel, as you read, as you elbow your way through crowds in the street or in a public meeting. Think about how your product could be used to advantage by those people.

5. NOTE WHAT YOUR COMPETITOR IS DOING in getting new business. Don't resent him. Outdo him. Reach out and score a million for yourself.

6. NUMEROUS PROSPECT SOURCES. Every customer, every acquaintance is a potential referral source for prospects. Cultivate all sources with HARD SELL PROSPECTING in mind.

7. ORGANIZE YOUR PROSPECT LIST. Use file cards. Use a notebook. Use anything you desire so long as it provides quick and ready reference for you. Now organize your work and SELL. In substance that is the Secret of the Magic Power in the Hard Sell in prospecting.

Tips for Gaining Buyer Confidence by Turning On Hard Sell Power

There was a time when you could pick a salesman out of the crowd. In the horse-and-buggy days, salesmen were referred to as "slickers," "dudes," and "drummers." The "slickers" and the "dudes" favored circus-checked jackets, peg-top trousers, glittering stick pins studded with diamonds or near-diamonds, and gold-plated watch chains that stretched across their vests, usually with a rabbit's foot attached.

The "drummer" type was different. He was conservative. He plugged along lugging sample cases from door to door. Usually he had a good story to tell. He was a likable fellow. He also got his share of the business. His buyers had confidence in him.

Today a successful salesman has mastered the art of inspiring men. This is one of the *Secrets of the Hard Sell*. He gains confidence in that way. By productive showmanship he captures the attention of prospective buyers. He opens fire on them with HARD SELL points that create interest in, and desire for, what he has to sell. This is the positive approach. It separates the "live" prospects from the doubtful ones. This is the secret of upgrading the image of salesmanship.

How do we improve our image? We have to get fired up about this challenging business of moving goods from production lines to consumers. We may even have to change our attitude toward our competitors. When you get to know a competitor, he really is not a bad fellow. Even if he were, you will gain nothing by dramatizing that fact. If you tear him down, you downgrade another salesman and this, in turn, dims the image of all salesmen. Our credo should be to build up, not to tear down. This is another secret of the HARD SELL.

It could be time, too, for a change in the way we have been handling the hard-to-handle customer. Argument with a customer is fruitless. It's a luxury you can't afford. If you win the argument, you are apt to lose the sale, also a friend. You may get satisfaction out of telling off an ornery prospect: it's more profitable to tame him. Try patting him on the shoulder. Try being kind to him. Try to understand his point of view. Try to win his confidence.

A prospect does not really become a qualified prospect until we have gained some measure of his confidence. When we make the initial approach, we try to determine if we have a "live" one. The direct approach is important at this point. The specific appeal has the greater HARD SELL POWER. A most successful salesman summed it up in the following three steps:

(a) Make a believer out of a doubtful prospect. Make a direct, specific proposal to him. For example: "I can guarantee delivery of a carload of this item in time for your spring opening. Can we put that into production for you now? This will assure you of having a big-volume, profitable seller for that event."

(b) Offer the buyer a choice. "Do you prefer this design or that?" This can bring a firm decision or it can lead into a new avenue of discussion which may lead to a larger scale.

(c) Make a specific offer. Make it so attractive that it is almost impossible to refuse.

Buyer confidence was defined by one top-of-the-ladder sales executive as a form of faith. "That buyer you are working on has got to believe in you before he will put his money on the line. Never let him down. That's the secret of developing buyer-confidence."

As a statesman, Daniel Webster had the ability to draw others to his way of thinking. This was salesmanship at its finest—HARD SELL if you please. Webster said: "Confidence is a thing not to be produced by compulsion. Men can't be forced into trust." This confirms again that a SECRET OF THE HARD SELL lies in the art of persuasion.

Consider these five simple, yet effective ways of gaining buyer confidence:

1. Concentrate on the big, important thing affecting your prospect.

2. Stress those things that you can show or dramatize for easy visualization.

3. Use statistics sparingly. Use them when you can

simplify them. Use them when you can relate them directly to your prospect. When you can make statistics important to your prospect then they become a valuable tool in the HARD SELL.

4. Know your product. Know its uses. Become a specialist in the uses of your product. Help your prospect profit or otherwise benefit by using your product. That's another secret of the HARD SELL.

5. Play it square. Grant no special discounts or favors to one prospect over another. Double dealing is a foe of the HARD SELL. It destroys the buyer's confidence.

The secret of gaining buyer confidence lies within yourself. Your enthusiasm is transmitted to your prospect. Your confidence in yourself and in your product is communicated to your prospect. Basically, you are striving to cause your prospect to want eagerly what you have to sell. That requires a combination of self-confidence and the HARD SELL.

I once overheard a conversation between a prospective buyer and a salesman that was most revealing. The prospect came into the store shopping for a sports jacket. He left after buying a sports jacket, a pair of slacks, and a complete suit. What happened? (a) Buyer confidence was developed. (b) The magic power of the HARD SELL was released in a quiet, pleasant, persuasive manner. Check the following steps that salesman took to close that triple sale:

Step No. 1.—He practically clinched the sports jacket deal, then laid the jacket aside.

Step No. 2.—He brought out three new suits and got the prospect interested in them. He got him to commit himself on which suit he liked best. He slipped the coat on the prospect. He edged his prospect over to the mirror and that was that.

Step No. 3.—"Let me call our tailor. I want him to give us his opinion of this suit. It looks so smart on you." With the tailor's "specialized" opinion added to the salesman's HARD SELL, sales resistance dropped to zero.

Step No. 4.—To the tailor: "While you're here, give us your idea about this sports jacket." Now he had a suit, a sports jacket and a pair of slacks involved. The tailor was making notes, smiling approval, and suggesting a few minor alterations.

Step No. 5.—That salesman wrapped up a package sale of four pieces of fine clothing instead of one as originally intended by the prospect. All this resulted from application of the *Secrets of the Hard Sell* plus the gaining of buyer confidence.

Mutual confidence might well include the seller-buyer relationship. Of this, the eminent jurist, Learned Hand, once stated:

"The mutual confidence on which all else depends can be maintained only by an open mind and a brave reliance upon free discussion."

Dollar Value in Friendship and How Secrets of the Hard Sell Make It Work

Friendship is so closely tied in with successful prospecting and selling that we often take it for granted. But, friendship also has a big dollar value. In one instance, a five-figure contract was at stake in a board meeting. The salesman who piloted his firm's bid for that choice bit of business seemed to be confident of the outcome. He and his competitors were waiting in the reception room for the board's decision. One by one they were called in. Finally the decision came. The confident salesman got the business. Why? One thing, he had two solid friends sitting on that board. "Everything else being equal I had that much edge on my competitors," that salesman told me. "I had two friends on the board. They owed me nothing but in a showdown I felt that they would be voting for me." To him the dollar value in friendship was obvious. To the board, however, the secret of why he was awarded the contract no doubt rested with the convincing quality of that salesman's HARD SELL presentation.

When friendship is allied with *Secrets of the Hard Sell* the dollar effect becomes magnetic. As Michel Montaigne, the French scholar and essayist, wrote: "Friendship is the highest degree of perfection in society." The dollar value of friendship stands out when we include it as one of the *Secrets of the Hard Sell*. Friendship gains its dollar value through the magic power in the HARD SELL.

As HARD SELL SPECIALISTS, interested in the dollar value of friendship, we might profit by this gentle tip from an educator, author and religious leader: John A. Widtsoe once said: "Your friends will pull you down or lift you up, therefore choose them carefully."

George Washington probably never had heard the term HARD SELL. But, when it came to rallying his forces to conquer the British he showed what the magic power of the HARD SELL can do in a crisis. On friendship, Washington had this to say: "Be courteous to all, but intimate with few; let those few be well tried before you give them your confidence. True friendship is a plant of slow growth."

Secrets of the Hard Sell cause friendship to have dollar value when we capitalize on the magic power in the following:

(a) Personal warmth.

(b) Sincere interest in others.

(c) Admiration of the accomplishments of others.

(d) Sincere appreciation.

(e) Sensitiveness to needs and wants of others.

(f) Unselfish, constructive attitude.

The dollar value in friendship in selling is linked with each of the foregoing possibilities for personal profit.

One of the most impressive HARD SELL presentations I have heard was made by an investment counselor. Speaking to a hand-picked group of prospects, he stressed only the significant points about the land mass that he was selling. I spoke to him later about his technique. This was his secret of the HARD SELL in prospecting and in selling:

1. "Talk about only the big, important things. I don't muddy the water with trivialities.

2. "I use statistics sparingly. When I do use them I cut them down to the meaningful 'bone.' I use statistics

as a tool in selling. I try to make statistics 'live.' I use statistics to prove a point. I use statistics to create mental images of how my product can become profitable to my prospects.

3. "I help my audience to comprehend the significance to them of my proposal. I clarify how my product works in use. I try to get my audience to visualize how my product can be used to benefit them.

4. "I use endorsements whenever I can get them. When someone endorses what I sell, the true dollar value of friendship is revealed."

Salesmen who are image-builders are friendship-builders. They are alert to create a favorable image for themselves, for their products, and for the firms they represent. There is dollar value in their attitudes. They are sincere. They radiate personal warmth. Add it up and you have quite a package of *Secrets of the Hard Sell* for prospecting and for closing sales.

One successful salesman built volume two ways: First, by combining dollar-value friendship with HARD SELL approaches in prospecting; second, by combining a pleasant, friendly, helpful attitude in the selling process. This man kept an up-to-date prospect list. He called it his "friendship directory." Here are some sources he explored to keep his friendship prospect list at its peak dollar-producing value:

1. Yellow pages in the telephone directory.
2. Chamber of Commerce business and industrial directors.
3. Newspapers and other advertising media.
4. Public records of business licenses, building permits, etc.
5. News stories in the local press.
6. Billboards, calendars, business cards, etc.
7. Office building directories.
8. Church and club directories.
9. City directories.
10. Programs of luncheon clubs.

Bill Factor sold a high quality candy. Going after new dealers he concentrated on his deluxe boxed line. He used it as a dollar-value friendship-builder in prospecting and in selling. Secretaries to dealer-executives knew him well. He was a bearer of sweet gifts. More than that, Bill was a sincere, pleasant, helpful fellow. He got in to see prospects where competitors often bumped against "busy" barriers. Bill made friends along the line. They had dollar value. Not just by leaving an occasional box of candy, but by being a friendly guy himself. Bill's attitude had dollar value in opening closed doors. When he succeeded in getting through those closed doors, he combined his sincere friendship with the *Secrets of the Hard Sell*. Result: Bill Factor's sales volume enjoyed a steady growth even against odds.

How to Convert Inquisitive Prospects into Buyers by the Magic Power in the Hard Sell

When your prospects begin asking questions you're lucky. A real estate salesman I know capitalizes on the inquisitiveness of people. To tease his inquisitive prospects, he cloaks his operation in mystery. He plays the super-secretive role. It's all designed to cause people to ask: "What's Jack up to now?" When that sort of inquisitiveness catches fire, it smokes out prospects who really want to find out what Jack is up to. To satisfy these inquisitive prospects, Jack presents an "unusual opportunity" for profit in real estate. He gives his proposals an appearance of freshness, of newness. He does this with HARD SELL POWER. He converts inquisitive prospects who come his way to become satisfied buyers. This all ties in with Jack's original objective: To score a million by prospecting with the magic power in *Secrets of the Hard Sell*.

Curiosity is a HARD SELL "product." "The important thing," said Albert Einstein, "is not to stop questioning. Curiosity has its own reason for existing."

The curiosity of a prospect, on which you can capitalize in selling, has similar influence on you. Creative sales people are inquisitive people. They ask. They dig. They want to know WHY and HOW. "Every man ought to be inquisitive through every hour of his great adventure down to the day when he shall no longer cast a shadow in the sun," according to Frank M. Colby, noted critic.

In mastering *Secrets of the Hard Sell,* you are drawn into the fascinating mysteries of how inquisitive prospects can be converted into buyers. You will find that the simplest of queries vibrate with hidden HARD SELL power. Consider these every-day questions that pop up:

(a) Have you noticed how the A,B,C, Advertising Agency is spreading out? Where do they find all those new clients? (Mystery, curiosity.)

(b) That organ you are demonstrating. What do you call it? How soon could I learn to play it? (Interest, curiosity.)

(c) Is this the new infrared oven they're talking about? What makes it better than the others? (Inquisitiveness.)

(d) They tell me those expensive draperies are fade-proof? How come? What makes them so? (Interest. Inquisitiveness.)

(e) A tape recorder? What possible use would I have for that? (Curiosity.)

(f) Why do so many people put so much money in life insurance? Why should I buy it? (Interest. Curiosity.)

(g) Why should I buy hospital insurance when I have Medicare? (Interest. Curiosity.)

CURIOSITY? The open door to a sale. From "a" to "g" we have curiosity being revealed by "live" prospects. The situation created by inquisitiveness expands until we have a thriving field of "live" prospects awaiting the harvest.

The foundation for building sales volume links two persuasive factors together. Here they are:

1. CURIOSITY. This is the "I'll take a look" attitude of the skeptical prospect.

2. INQUISITIVENESS. This is the revealing attitude of the "I want to be shown" prospect.

Both the curious prospect and the inquisitive prospect are "live" prospects. To convert them into buyers, three tested methods present themselves to MASTERS OF THE HARD SELL. Here they are:

(1) ORIGINALITY IN PRESENTATION. This involves rising above drab approaches. It challenges us to spell out to our prospects HOW and WHY they can benefit by buying from us. In itself, this is the most interesting presentation we can make. It has, or can have, direct emotional appeal with the magic of HARD SELL POWER in it.

(2) THE SECRET of the conversion of a prospect into a buyer in many cases is the arousing of curiosity. The automobile industry is a good example. Producers of new models go after prospects by creating anticipation long before the new model is unveiled in dealers' showrooms. Masters of the HARD SELL ride the crest of this wave of inquisitiveness. They convert inquisitive prospects into buyers.

A new food product is presented with accent on ease-in-preparation. Prospects are invited to taste the prepared product. They are told about the subtle flavor. They taste it again. They now become "live," more inquisitive prospects. Soon the magic power in the *Secrets of the Hard Sell* grabs them. They become buyers. On such persuasive foundations are sales records written up.

(3) DRAMATIC DEMONSTRATION. This employs any device that injects life into the product. A moving object has more interest than something stationary. Syrup becomes more appetizing if you see it being poured. Clothing has more sell-power when worn than spread flat on a table. An automobile engine with a quiet soothing hum becomes more interesting than if we just point our finger at it. A food freezer becomes more salable if we pull frozen food out of it than if we show an empty freezing compartment.

Curiosity and inquisitiveness are stimulated by presentations that are original in concept and by "live" demonstrations. These are among the secrets of scoring a million begun by HARD SELL PROSPECTING.

Hard Sell Secrets of Getting Paid for Waiting Time

Among the best trained people I have met are the secretaries and receptionists who guard the passageways to important people

I have wanted to see. Almost all of them have challenged the most determined salesmen I have known. These guardians of executive portals largely determine whether you are smart enough to get paid for waiting time. They set the stage. You make the decision.

A man named Fred Perkins solved the waiting-time problem in a singular way. I studied his method. I witnessed him at a receptionist's desk one day. He handled the delay or brushoff problem something like this:

> *Receptionist:* "Mr. Barton is tied up at this time. I'm sorry about your appointment. That's disappointing, I know, and I have no idea how long he'll be tied up. Do you wish to wait or shall I set up another appointment?"
>
> *Fred:* "In a way this is a break for me. I'm a busy man, but I'll just sit down here and work out something that I know Mr. Barton is anxious to see." Fred takes a seat, opens his brief case and pulls out an impressive file. The secretary's eyes roll in his direction. In a few minutes Fred gets up, tucks the file under his arm and quietly approaches the receptionist. He asks: "Can you tell me if a Mr. Atwood has been here this morning?" (Atwood was a competitor of Fred.) The receptionist replies: "Yes, Mr. Atwood is with Mr. Barton right now."

This was disturbing but valuable information for Fred. He quickly revised his planned approach. He was familiar with Atwood's technique. Trailing an aggressive competitor almost demanded that Fred move in with a tempting, solid proposal. With time already given to Atwood, Fred hardly expected to waste even a minute of Mr. Barton's time. But, with a HARD SELL approach, with a quick, colorful presentation loaded with self-interest angles Fred believed he could make headway with Mr. Barton. Fred also figured he could do better by getting to Mr. Barton at once, even behind his competitor, than to try later. He told the receptionist he would wait. When Atwood came out, Fred was encouraged by his competitor's solemn expression. Fred did succeed in landing that piece of business. He got well paid for his waiting time.

A SECRET OF THE HARD SELL becomes evident in that one case involving a decision of whether to wait or not. The secret is the part secretaries and receptionists play in the success and failure of sales people. Sales people profit by "selling themselves" to secretaries and receptionists. This is an area for skill in the HARD SELL.

After several days' effort to break through barriers, an industrial property salesman succeeded in getting a limited time interview with a fully qualified and desirable prospect. This prospect's secretary accompanied the salesman into the executive's office. She said: "I have granted this gentleman five minutes to see you. You have another appointment in 10 minutes." Quickly the salesman placed his watch on the executive's desk, "I will hold to five minutes," the salesman said pleasantly. In those five minutes, he placed a brief, carefully prepared outline of his proposal before his prospect. His prospect was interested. He began asking questions. The salesman interrupted him. "My five minutes are up," he said. His prospect nodded a pleasant response. A luncheon engagement for the next day was made. Other appointments followed. Eventually a sale was closed. This edged that salesman toward his goal: Scoring a million in sales. He, too, had learned the HARD SELL SECRET of getting paid for waiting time.

Secrets of the 12-Hour Prospecting Campaign

Three factors are involved in your attempt to score a million. Let's examine them as they apply to you directly:

1. TIME—Elusive, yet manageable.
2. YOUR PRODUCT—Worthy of your finest HARD SELL effort.
3. YOU—The energy department which produces imaginative, creative, dynamic, HARD SELL IDEAS for marketing your product.

The basis of productive selling is systematic, penetrating prospecting. By this you can aspire to score a million.

In time-management you activate your resourcefulness. You stand on your own feet. You lean on nobody. You become your own man. One salesman in the five-year service class saw the picture of his future quite clearly. He saw challenging possibilities. He zeroed in on scoring a million. He set a deadline for hitting that million objective. He made it sooner. He out-sold his original dead-line. He did this by skillful management of himself and of his time. He began with time. He set up a 12-hour-day, 5-day-week schedule. He broke this schedule into six time segments, as follows:

8 a. m. to 9 a. m.—Setting up the day's appointments. Setting up a schedule of "cold turkey" calls. Setting up a schedule for prospecting.

9 a. m. to 11 a. m.—Recheck of morning calls. Reappraise prospects called upon. Reappraise sales made. "Did I do as well as could have been done by releasing more of the magic power in the HARD SELL?"

12 m. to 1:30 p. m.—Lunch and relax.

1:30 p. m. to 5 p. m.—Make HARD SELL scheduled calls, "cold turkey" calls, and do prospecting.

5 p. m. to 6 p. m.—Evaluation of the day. Set up objectives for tomorrow. Homeward bound.

With that schedule, that salesman achieved his major objectives. He also had time to study uses of his product. Through study he came up with fresh ideas for the profitable use of his product by his prospects and his customers. That schedule for a productive day leaves a flexible margin for your 12-hour schedule. There's time to join in family fun. There's time for community service. There's time for self-improvement. The salesman who set that pace for himself maintained enthusiasm for his work. He accomplished all this by skillful, enjoyable, profitable time-management.

3

Stirring Up Buying Fever
in Prospects with
the Hard Sell

Here's a tip that can bring you untold riches: *Harness the magic power in Secrets of the Hard Sell by riding rough shod over anything that would discourage you.*

I recall a young salesman who put this principle to a stern test. Two years after he plunged into selling life insurance he was crippled in an automobile accident. He lost one leg. Well-meaning associates urged him to give up selling and seek employment as a desk man. He refused to listen. Instead he raised his sights. He set up "impossible" goals to reach for. In two years he had worked out an annual income of about $8,000 with two legs. Now, although "handicapped," he saw greater returns ahead. With only one leg and artificial devices, he began climbing. He passed $15,000, went on to $25,000 and continued on to the million dollar club and still saw greater possibilities in his future. He accomplished this by harnessing the magic power in *Secrets of the Hard Sell!*

You, too, can capitalize on these four requirements for success in selling:

1. BELIEVE in yourself. BELIEVE in what you have to sell. BELIEVE in what it can do for others.

2. CULTIVATE SELF-DETERMINATION. Crush discouragement. Think and believe in HARD SELL SUCCESS.

3. PRACTICE SELF CONTROL. Welcome resistance as a fresh challenge. Tackle obstacles knowing you are capable of rising above them.

4. DEVELOP SELF CONFIDENCE. Feed your driving power. This is the fuel of success which is one of the elements in the *Secrets of the Hard Sell*.

As it was in the case of the "handicapped" insurance salesman, you, too, will meet well-meaning "play it cool" friends. If you permit these fellows to succeed in unharnessing the magic power of the HARD SELL they will kill sales for you.

An aggressive and successful investment salesman labeled the "play it cool" advocates as "worry merchants." He said that if he had listened to such gloom peddlers he would have fallen far short of his objectives. Instead of "playing it cool" he adopted a "go-get 'em" spirit. As a result he shot his monthly income up from a few hundred dollars to round out an annual income of more than $50,000.

Consider those two cases we have discussed here. In them we have evidence that self-mastery plus mastery of the *Secrets of the Hard Sell* go hand in hand.

Let's examine the other side of the "play it cool" coin: I walked into the office of a successful advertising salesman. He was seated near a window gazing out over part of his market. "I'm about to tackle some of the toughest prospects I've ever met," he said, looking at me with a determined spark in his eye. "I've been sitting here planning and putting a jig saw puzzle together. I've decided to go after the toughest account out there in that area I can see from this window. *If* I land that account, *and I will,* I can add 100 percent to my commission check."

That salesman was thinking big. He was reaching out to harness the magic power in *Secrets of the Hard Sell*. And, he did sell that "fat" account. He also went on to close other "fat" accounts in that same area. He continued to make his income go up, up, and up. He believed in himself. Never doubting. He was determined to succeed. He knew he could. He was in firm control of himself and of his line. He was aware of his own weaknesses as well as his own strength. Then, to cap it all, he possessed that greatest of virtues in selling: He was self-confident. Not arrogant. Just a humble self-confidence, which gave him magic power in the HARD SELL. By this he enjoyed the richness of selling. He took the persuasive steps to stir up buying fever in his prospects. And, they liked it. They bought. All of this dominant power is embodied in the *Secrets of the Hard Sell.*

Secret of Generating Hard Sell Power to Set Higher Sales Records

We hear a great deal about technology and other matters pertinent to modern progress. Too often as salesmen we get unduly tangled up in such highly technical subjects. The secret of generating HARD SELL POWER need not be overly complicated. Nor should it be. In the HARD SELL you are concerned with two people. You are concerned with how they will react in a given situation. The two people in question are *You* and *Your Prospect.* In a selling situation nobody else really matters. Now let us say "it's your move." We believe that your prospect will respond favorably to a presentation that promises benefits to him personally. Your job is to convince him that this is true. It may be more difficult to get him excited about the complexities of a technical problem. The latter, however, may be vitally important to him. The HARD SELL point is that it does not click as an appeal to personal interest clicks. But, that vital point can be covered later, probably with HARD SELL effect. The appeal that hits at your prospect's heart and his pocketbook comes first. It contains the magic power of HARD SELL and your primary mission at this point is to generate enough HARD SELL POWER to sway the thinking of your prospect in your favor. Too often we are tempted to slip into an involved technical discussion which may weaken our big opportunity for a HARD SELL thrust.

Consider the following seven secrets of big-time producers in selling:

1. SMILE. Radiate warmth and personal interest in your prospect.

2. BE AT EASE. Nervousness is contagious. Set your prospect at ease, too.

3. GET ORGANIZED. Have a specific and appealing idea to present.

4. ASK QUESTIONS. Let your prospect do most of the talking at first. Often he does a swell job of selling himself, *If* he is properly led.

5. PRAISE YOUR PROSPECT. Praise mellows him. Praise him for his judgment. Praise him for his accomplishments. Make him feel important.

6 LISTEN. Many of us talk too much. You can learn much if you listen well. Thomas Hobbes, British philosopher, pointed out that knowledge is power. Acquiring knowledge is one secret of generating HARD SELL POWER.

7 SAY "THANKS." Show sincere appreciation for a customer's business. Sincere appreciation has HARD SELL POWER.

The Nudge Also Has Hard Sell Power.—A salesman with an envious record said the gentle nudge can often swing the deal. "Often a nudge is all that is needed to get a reluctant prospect to buy," he said. "Take my own record," he added. "I *simplify* selling as much as I can. I try to find out what a prospect wants or what he needs. Then I go into action to make it easy for him to get it."

Another master of the HARD SELL showed me his record to prove that HARD SELL POWER can be generated. "My business is to sell," he emphasized. "When I get my teeth into a situation I take a bulldog grip on it and hang on. A live prospect and a product on which I am thoroughly sold myself present a challenge to me. I go after that business tenaciously. Not just to be tenacious but to persuasively guide that prospect toward an irresistible desire to buy from me. I believe a salesman's first step should be to sell himself to his prospect. He can't do a good job at that unless he has sold himself on himself. This is the principle: I must be convinced that I am the man best qualified to sell my products to my prospects."

George Romney had the HARD SELL principles down pat.

He established a high production record in the automobile field. Mr. Romney made this point: "A measure of success is not a question of judging yourself as compared to somebody else, but a question of judging yourself against your own potential."

The secret of generating HARD SELL POWER is to do your best today and then to beat that record tomorrow.

How the Magic Power of the Hard Sell Crushes Sales Resistance

Over their coffee cups salesmen often chat about stubborn prospects. In most of these bull sessions one principle glitters like a gem in the darkness. That principle is this:

"The most stubborn resistance usually wilts when the salesman takes command."

Sales are lost when prospects are permitted to take over.

Sales are closed when salesmen stand firm. Then, and only then, do they subdue resistance with the maximum persuasive power in the HARD SELL.

A discerning and successful tire distributor praised one persistent salesman for his refusal to back up and his persistence in presenting the whole captivating story of the products he sold. "I have found it to be most productive to me to turn you down flat," he said. "When I do that I see the fullness of your selling ability. You make your pitch. You do that well. But, when I shake my head and close the book, then you really get into action. With a flat turn down you quit sparring. You stop fumbling. You hit straight at what concerns me most. Your presentation now becomes more colorful. You're at high pitch when you close and ask for the order. Why don't you go into action right off the bat? You're a great salesman when I put up stiff resistance. I like that."

In that one experience, that salesman discovered the magic power of the HARD SELL. He discovered that the HARD SELL gets business and also wins the admiration of those who buy. He also discovered how sales resistance can be crushed by it. As he later confessed, he learned much from a friendly, interested customer who was impressed by the HARD SELL. He later detected that prospects and customers alike enjoy a colorful HARD SELL presentation. They became enthusiastic about what he had to sell because he was enthusiastic. They bought because he had thoroughly sold them by the magic power in the HARD SELL.

Sales resistance can be a leisurely trap for salesmen as well as being a formidable barrier. There are those who are "gun shy" when prospects rear up against them. They become overly courteous, submissive in fact, and pleasantly evasive. They are the soft-spoken "let's think this over" type of salesmen. They are vulnerable subjects for prospects who habitually object and resist buying. Masters of the HARD SELL have proven by their own production records that the most vigorous sales resistance can be broken down by bold selling—THE HARD SELL.

A specialty salesman I knew had been warned about a prospect who fell into the evasive category. That salesman moved in on that prospect with a firm, direct, and specific approach. In minutes he had the prospect talking freely about his business. He was revealing to the salesman many ways in which the salesman's products could be beneficial to him. Before the interview concluded, that salesman had applied the magic power of the HARD SELL and had a substantial contract in his pocket for an aggressive merchandising campaign with TV commercials. By his HARD SELL approach that salesman had swept that evasive prospect off his feet. This is how he did it and how you, in a similar situation, can do it:

(a) He first captured his prospect's interest by tempting him with prospects of making money.

(b) He showed his prospect how he could do it.

(c) He proved his point by showing his prospect how others had made money by the same sort of campaign proposed by the salesman.

This was all incorporated in the magic power of the HARD SELL. It was the HARD SELL IN ACTION. The prospect enjoyed it. He wanted to profit. So he quit resisting an idea and he finally succumbed to overwhelming, persuasive pressure and he bought. . . . The salesman also profited. Mutual confidence had resulted from HARD SELL COMMUNICATION which crushed the sales resistance.

How to Create Presentations That Are
Alive with Inducements to Buy

Dynamic, convincing presentations are a combination of three things:

1. TELLING
2. SHOWING
3. DEMONSTRATING

The demonstration becomes the clincher in a selling situation. You tell, then you show, and then you deliver the punch that either fizzles or puts over your idea and your product. You have sold your prospect on how he can benefit by taking on what you have to sell. To accomplish this feat requires showmanship. It places you in the spotlight as an actor of sorts. We, as salesmen, may be "hams" on the stage but we can still put dramatic power into our presentations if we believe in ourselves and in what we have to sell.

A toy salesman stirred up a wild rush for one of his products by becoming a showman. He walked through a department store pulling an *Alive-like* toy behind him. The attraction was a wooden clown bobbing up and down. The drama was a poker-faced salesman with a string in his fingers pulling behind him a wooden clown bobbing up and down. Kids yelled for the toy. Women giggled. Men pulled out their wallets.

That wholesale toy salesman had been turned down when he attempted to sell that toy to the management of that store. But that salesman had now demonstrated the profit-value in that toy. The dealer bought that toy in quantity simply because that salesman created a presentation that was alive with buying power. He had to do this to overcome the cool reception his first undramatic presentation received. Restless creativity was the secret of how that salesman built volume sales for himself and for toy dealers.

Case records are full of instances where a prospect was sold, or could have been sold, by interest-demanding presentation. This recalls the attitude of a salesman who seemed to have a knack for selling to "dead" prospects. At one time I worked under that man's supervision. I appealed for help from him on one occasion. I had hit a discouraging low. I was losing confidence. I poured out my woes to that man as we drove along. He stopped in a warehouse district. "They are all dead here," I suggested. He smiled. The shocker for me was that my tutor signed up three beautiful orders before the morning was over. Those orders came from what I called "dead" prospects. "What profit is there in burning up gas to get somewhere else when you haven't made a decent bid for business right here?" he had asked me before he called on the first "dead" prospect. Ever since then, his business-getting remark has stuck in my mind: "Might as well park right here."

Sales are made by dynamic presentations. How to create them? Here is one way:

(a) Make your presentation *live*. Show how your product can be profitably used. Animate wherever possible.

(b) Begin by capturing attention. That achieved, never let go. Maintain the tempo of your presentation. Keep it alive. Keep it moving toward a successful close.

(c) Make your presentation pertinent to the best interests of your prospect. Show him how to use your product in his business. Show him how to profit by taking on your product. Make your proposal alluring, factual, colorful, believable.

(d) Prove your claims for your product with unimpeachable evidence—case records, endorsements, and the like.

The foregoing "a" to "d" steps have HARD SELL power. Each of those steps is easy, smooth, direct in operation. With a RESTLESS CREATIVITY dominating your attitude toward getting more business, you really can restore life to "dead" prospects. By maintaining that attitude those same "dead" prospects will never "die" again.

"Silent" presentations also have HARD SELL power.

A representative for a motivational institute made this effective presentation: He placed a neat, easy-to-read portfolio on the desk of the general manager of a prospective account. "Here are some of your friends. I thought you might be interested in what they are doing. Several of them are in the same business as you are. They find our service profitable in many ways. Take a look at the list."

With that bit of unspectacular HARD SELL the salesman stood by in silence. Finally, his prospect invited him to sit down. He began asking questions of the salesman. HARD SELL silence at the right time has opened the door to landing a much-desired account. The preparation of the portfolio and the confident manner of presentation made it *alive with wanting-to-buy* power. All this was the result of careful planning and RESTLESS CREATIVITY, which is the No. 1 SECRET OF THE HARD SELL.

Long-Range Hard Sell Power in the Magic of Good Will

Friendship in business? Of course. In the real estate business it is often referred to as the "blue sky" value of the price of commercial property. Corporations in various fields set up formidable budgets for what is called "public relations"—an impressive label for "good will," or just plain "friendship."

Salesmen who take a long range view of their operation understand the magic power in good will. They have proved its potency as a HARD SELL tool.

Friendship sweetens a business transaction. A sale closed with a firm handclasp leaves the welcome mat out for a return HARD SELL presentation. That good will is predicated, however, on the future performance of the salesman and the product which he sold.

Secrets of the HARD SELL that have run up sales volume in virtually every line on the market draw their potency from the binding, yet challenging and demanding ties of good will.

Public confidence in a product is a symbol of good will toward the makers of that product. Brand names known as symbols of quality are examples of product confidence. There is an element of good will in this. That product confidence or good will has been created and maintained by a long range vision of the HARD SELL power in the magic of good will.

Buyer confidence in you as a salesman is closely related to certain ties of friendship. It is a symbol of trust. Such buyers have faith in their favorite salesman. Those salesmen have earned that confidence. In no other way than through fidelity and integrity could they retain that good will. So long as that situation prevails, the magic power of good will holds sway. It opens the doors of opportunity for the HARD SELL to get in its mightiest blows. The effect of good will extends beyond the bartering counter. It is a soothing, yet productive, force in the hardest of all HARD SELL situations. Good will is an intangible asset of great worth.

A salesman whose record indicates that he has found one solution to the "no" problem takes this slant on flat rejections: He admits that when a prospect turns him down he is tempted to pull in his horns and retire. But, instead, he has learned to take the turn-down as an invitation to do a better job of HARD SELLING. This makes the "no" a challenge. It dares him to win. This, of course, leads him nearer to a solution of the "no" problem. He moves in with a smile for a renewed HARD SELL thrust at the unsold prospect. He changes direction. He smiles at the defeat he has suffered. He agrees with the prospect's objection. This is disarming. Then, in effect, he says: "I'm glad you brought that up. That's a great angle. It reminds me of what your friend down the street is doing." This again diverts the prospect's attention from saying "no" to "let's see what that guy down the street is up to." All this, and more, is done with a smile. The principle: Mix the HARD SELL with liberal portions of good will. Keep smiling. Follow through and hang on!

Another energetic HARD SELL traveling man built a com-prehensive and profitable list of hardware dealer accounts. His name became a household word among dealers. They believed in him. He was their problem-solver. The dealers phoned him when their problems got burdensome. In many cases, they virtually per-mitted him to write their orders. They trusted him. The reason: *They profited by taking his advice.*

But, what about that HARD SELL salesman? With all that confidence placed upon him, his personal burden was increased. Nevertheless, he profited along with his customers. Through the magic power of good will he held a firm HARD SELL grip on his accounts. Together they did a flourishing business.

In time, another salesman stepped in to take over those ac-counts that the previous salesman had developed in his own good will way. In time, that new salesman lost those accounts. Why? He failed to recognize the HARD SELL power in good will. He concentrated on the immediate sale. He overlooked the long range HARD SELL POWER in good will.

Another master of the HARD SELL with a liberal dose of the magic of good will was in the food products business. He sold to some who had been called "dead beats" by others. Interesting, too: his volume among those "dead beat" accounts continued to grow. His gains held firm. Here was his secret as he unburdened it to me:

1. "I try to create a customer, not just make a sale.

2. "I refrain from bragging. My customers are the most important people I know.

3. "I never forget a buyer. I watch for opportunities to do something for him, not to him. I check back on every order to see that it comes through O.K.

4. "I never knowingly mislead a customer. They're too hard to come by to deceive.

5. "I neither knock nor boost my competitor. I just concentrate on my customers, their welfare, how I can better serve them, especially with my products.

6. "I refuse to be tempted by shady deals for an easy buck.

7. "On the phone I aim to be a diplomat. Telephone sharpness can be a killer of business."

At the top of the list of little known HARD SELL steps to stir up buying power in prospects is that intangible known as friendship. As Charles Fletcher Dole told an audience:

"Good will is the mightiest practical force in the universe."

4

How to Turn Cold Calls into Hot Sales Producers Through the Hard Sell

One SECRET of finding hot prospects for what you have to sell lies in the MAGIC HARD SELL POWER in "cold turkey" calls.

A "cold turkey" call often turns out to be your great adventure in selling. In "cold turkey" calls you become an explorer of the unknown.

The SECRETS of success in "cold turkey" calls have been extracted from the accomplishments of successful salesmen. With them, triple objectives are common. Three steps have proved to be sales producers. Study these three tested steps. Prepare to employ them in your "cold turkey" calls. Prepare yourself to go in with HARD SELL power. Here is your three-step chart:

(1) GO IN TO SELL.—Cold calls warrant more than a "hello, how are you" treatment. Your prospects probably will be as disappointed as you if your calls wind up as hand-shaking events. The moment you make your appearance your prospect's self-interest is turned on. He anticipates that you are there to sell something. If you present an idea that can prove profitable to him, you have his attention. Otherwise, he begins to figure out how he

can get rid of you. Basically your prospects are selfish people. So are you. If you go to those prospects with no idea of how to grab their interest you are cheating them. You are also cheating yourself. The least you could have done was to have flashed a hot, persuasive idea. Your first step in a "cold turkey" call is to open up with a sales pitch that suggests to your prospect: "This is loaded with personal benefits for you." Proceed from that point, step by step, to clinch a first-call sale. No better way has been found than to show a prospect how to make money out of your idea.

(2) GO IN TO SERVE.—Get out of your dugout. Get over on your prospect's side. See the picture from his viewpoint. Expect that he will resist buying. Try to answer his objections before he voices them. Show him how you can steer him into money-making. Suggest ways for him to have more fun. Show him how he can enjoy more leisure through the benefits afforded by the product you have for sale. Create a mental picture of how he can benefit from your product or service. Appealing to his self-interest will register with him. He's by nature a selfish person. His own self-interest makes him vulnerable. Because you, too, are selfish you will turn on your most persuasive self to induce your prospect to buy. With an attitude of desire to serve, you will warm up your prospect. You show him how you and the house you represent can serve him with profit to him. When you convince him that these benefits can be his, you have insured two-way communication. Effective communication is one of the *Secrets of the Hard Sell*. The result: A sale today and more sales coming up.

(3) GO IN TO CREATE A LOYAL CUSTOMER.—A strange HARD SELL POWER is present in "cold turkey" calls. This power is two-way communication which leaves the buyer excited about the purchase he has made. Much more can be accomplished in a "cold turkey" call than snatching an order from the prospect's fingers and getting out of sight before he changes his mind. Take time to listen to your prospect. Take time to listen to a customer. Take time to serve. "Cold turkey" calls become hot sales producers when they result in mutual confidence from which sales result.

Fundamentally, cold-call selling amounts to beating the bushes to get prospects out in the open. One SECRET of cold call success is to sell on the first call. Each call can be an exciting adventure in creative selling. It should be! It's a natural as a laboratory for testing your own selling plans.

CHALLENGE OF THE COLD CALL: You are nearing your prospect's door. He may be tough. He may be a smiling, easy-going chap. You really don't know. You have only slight knowledge of his business. You think he should be able to use your product to advantage, but you really don't know. Now, you've opened his door. You blue-print the man the moment you see him. You're creating a mental image of the man. You're typing him. Your prospect probably is doing the same with you. He's sizing you up. Now, how about your first impression of your prospect? Was it about right? Wrong? You'll find out when you try to employ your selling skill on him. Obviously you should go in to sell, but you should be well prepared.

You may become ruffled if you are delayed in getting to your prospect. At times such delays are a godsend. "Cooling your heels" gives you time to listen and observe. A gabby secretary or warehouse clerk may reveal much to you that can be turned to your advantage. In waiting time you may pick up bits of information that clue you in on the type of man you are about to meet. Even expressions on the faces of those coming out of your prospect's office may tip you off on the climate beyond that closed door. At this point you may suffer temporary loss of enthusiasm for meeting your prospect. Or, you may become more eager than ever to get on with the battle.

While waiting one question may shoot through your hyper-sensitive brain. This is the question: "What right have I to invade that fellow's private domain?" That's a reasonable question. There is also this logical answer for it: "JUSTIFY YOUR PRESENCE!"

Fear plays a big part in the drama of waiting to see an unknown prospect. Some of us quiver at the thought of tackling a "big shot." But, some of us have learned that "small fry" are often more difficult than the top echelon. One case in point relates to an army recruit and an officer. The officer in this case was trying to "sell" the idea of military courtesy. The recruit had failed to salute. "Haven't you been taught to salute officers?" the recruit was asked. "Yes, sir," he replied, "but I haven't seen any yet." The officer maintained his cool. He smiled and said: "Well, soldier, I'm just a brigadier general. Here comes a second lieutenant. Look out!" And so it is in selling. As we crash gates in making "cold turkey" calls, we meet both generals and lieutenants.

The Principle: The cold call can be one test of a selling plan in action. It requires persistence and skill. Systematic use of the cold call makes it productive. Basic requirements: Knowledge of your product and its uses. Understanding of people and human motives. Self-confidence. Courage. Integrity. Quick thinking. Most of these skills can be acquired by self-disciplined application. Because cold call skill does have MAGIC HARD SELL POWER it is worth developing.

Have Fun and Reap Profits
Through the Magic in Cold Calls

An insurance executive once revealed to me a new wrinkle in profiting by the magic in cold calls. In this case there were two objectives. First, there was the matter of office morale and production. Second, the potentials for the sales staff. Here is how it was done:

> His insurance firm inaugurated "mass coffee breaks." Twice daily, business in the office came to a halt—once in the morning, once in the afternoon. Customers or potential customers who might be in the office at that time were invited to join the staff for snacks and refreshments. The "free snack" word got around. "Drop ins" picked up. This worried management. Salesmen were pleased. Their sales increased.
>
> One salesman who saw possibilities in the snack idea said: "Every drop in is a perfect set-up for making a cold call. I closed a sale last week that doubled my normal take for the month. I met that prospect when he was invited to join us for a snack. Perfect! At that point I took over. I followed through. This was fun. It was also profitable. He has developed into a choice account. Others on our staff are also having fun meeting people who join our snack-time crowd. They pick up live prospects and make 'cold calls' on the spot. It has turned out to be a new twist for me in making

cold calls. First, we set 'em up with a free snack. Then we cultivate them. By good selling we land them. I feel that I perform a real service for those I meet in this way. I also profit by many routine calls which have seldom produced very little in sales results."

Cold calls need not be confined to door-bell ringing or rapping on guarded office doors. Cold calls can be those in which you break through the social crust. Whenever you meet someone for the first time, you have a "cold call" opportunity. It might be in a snack bar, on a bus, in a crowded elevator, or at a public meeting. If you are alert, it could mean a live prospect to be developed. This is the strange HARD SELL power in cold calls.

A luggage salesman consistently outsells his associates. He told me that he allots himself a fixed number of daily cold calls to be made. On each of these calls he tries to release the magic power in *Secrets of the Hard Sell*. His daily cold call quota system contributed to jacking up his income into the five-figure class. This man innovates. He uses HARD SELL showmanship. I recall when his firm came out with a new idea in briefcase design. He received the usual photographs. He received the usual "how to use" drawings. But, that salesman thought beyond that. To him that briefcase had HARD SELL possibilities. Being sold on it himself, why shouldn't he use it? What stronger recommendation could he present? Result: Prospects, cold call and all, got interested in the new briefcase he was carrying. Their interest intensified when he opened it up. It became an immediate conversation piece when he used it in his presentations. That salesman made his briefcase more than a product sample. He made it a showpiece in action. This HARD SELL approach perked up buyers in office supply houses. They were tempted. The new design, the multiple utility features had profit possibilities for those buyers. They observed and listened as that salesman demonstrated his briefcase in use. All this added to that salesman's fun in selling. By the simple device of carrying and using his product that luggage salesman made his cold calls pay off. He exploited his product by making it tempting to prospects.

That luggage salesman appealed to the self-interest of his

prospects. Either they wanted a briefcase like the one he was carrying or they wanted to buy them for resale. In either case he profited. In either case they benefited.

The SECRET of that salesman's success was the magic in cold calls plus the magic power in the HARD SELL. The principle is quite simple: (a) Make every cold call a HARD SELL call. (b) Make cold calls every day. (c) Tell your selling story dramatically. (d) Be persuasive whenever you meet live prospects. (e) Be alert for new prospects. They abound in clubs, in meetings, in stock exchanges, in factories, in retail stores, even in homes. Wherever you meet new people the possibility for a productive cold call exists. The SECRET: Get to know that person you meet for the first time. He may become your prime account by the end of the month if you follow through with *Secrets of the Hard Sell.*

Brew a Tonic with the Magic Ingredients in Cold Calls to Fortify Your Self-Confidence

Note these three ingredients in "cold turkey calls" which have magic sales power:

(1) SURPRISE.—This is the HARD SELL ingredient. Ralph Waldo Emerson said: "Nothing astounds men so much as common sense and plain dealing." Surprise snaps your sales presentation out of the ordinary and gives it life. Surprise may even put your prospect in a receptive mood. By achieving surprise you can release your full persuasive power in a tight sales situation.

A skillful salesman once boasted to me that he had never been caught by surprise. A few weeks later he retracted that statement. A prospect who was on the verge of buying suddenly changed his mind. He coldly dismissed my friend, offering no explanation. Next day my friend returned to that prospect. He was surprised by the pleasant reception he got. Not desiring to be caught off guard again my friend told me that he played it cool. He avoided any reference to his prospect's previous change of mind. However, the prospect reopened the case. To my friend he said: "I surprised you yesterday. You haven't surprised me today. I expected you to come back." Then he offered this explanation: "Yesterday I suddenly recalled that I had not checked out three claims you made for your product and your firm. I had intended to check those claims. I did not want to third-degree you. I was sure that if I did you would give me the usual company answer to my questions. I would have been surprised if you hadn't. So I just cut you off and went on my way to check out those three points. Your claims held water. They were perfectly solid. I was satisfied. Now I'm ready to buy. I suppose that surprises you. But, when you walked through that door a few minutes ago I was not surprised. You see, you knew, and I found out, that you had been on the level with me. So, I was pretty sure you would be back."

Major surprises in selling are often based on common sense.

(2) INQUISITIVENESS.—Be informed. Search for facts about your product and about your prospects. Be inquisitive. Encourage your prospects to be inquisitive. A question from a prospect opens the door for you to strike your HARD SELL licks. Inquisitiveness often saves you from losing a sale. Be armed with facts. The earnest and inquisitive prospect usually is half sold. His inquisitiveness indicates interest. Handle that prospect's inquisitiveness with HARD SELL SKILL and you will sell.

(3) ANTICIPATION.—There is excitement in anticipation. Your prospect's face lights up with excitement. He (or she) becomes anxious. He (or she) reaches out to examine what you have to sell. There is anticipation in his (or her) actions. There you have evidence that the seed of desire, which you planted, has taken root. You have caused your prospect to anticipate receiving wanted benefits. His self-interest has been aroused. You nourish it. You satisfy your prospect's expectancy. You show how benefit after benefit can be obtained on the easiest of terms. Anticipation is the prelude to excitement. This leads to closing the sale.

The foregoing trio of ingredients can be brewed into a tonic for stimulating your HARD SELL POWER. Jar your prospect into becoming more deeply involved in the selling process. In that way you capitalize on the element of surprise. This is also true if you can please or satisfy your prospect. Dramatize your product to capitalize on the surprise element. If you surprise your prospect by introducing a special feature or a new development, anticipate questions. Those questions indicate you have scored. They indicate interest. It's your move now—toward closing the sale. Here's the reason: When you combine all of those HARD SELL elements you arouse anticipation in the mind of your prospect. Dynamic presentations create SURPRISE. They stimulate INQUISITIVENESS. They arouse ANTCIPATION. The impact is reflected in your prospect's reaction. The cumulative effect is what sells goods and services.

Emerson, who reminded us of the magic power of common sense, also reminded us of the magic power in a thought. "Beware," he wrote, "when the great God lets loose a thinker on this planet."

William H. Wood, of the National Research Bureau, placed salesmen in the category of "professionals." And, why not? As he said: "Practically everything has to be sold. Religion and the Bible must be sold to doubters."

Doubters are sales barriers in other lines, too. Doubt is an obstacle to closing sales. Skillful salesmen batter away to knock doubt out of the sales picture. An insurance salesman I know is a highly rated producer. He said: "If I could get rid of the doubters I would have it made."

An automobile salesman with an enviable record of closing sales said: "I lost a sale the other day simply because I wasn't able to convince a guy that this car would be his best buy. He went away still in doubt. I should have finished my job. I should have sold him."

Is it possible to cope with doubt? Is it possible to overcome all sales barriers? Perhaps each of us in the "professional" sample case crowd has his own way of handling the doubt barrier. Mr. Wood offered this suggestion: "Good salesmanship requires skill, experience and hard work . . . knowledge of product and a proven, successful selling plan." That simplifies it to some extent. The *Secrets of the Hard Sell* meet most of those requirements. Skill results from persistent BOLD SELLING. By constantly testing the *Secrets of the Hard Sell* we get experience. Each sale we close adds to our experience. Each sale we lose adds to our experience. Perhaps the latter is our most valuable experience.

Like the triple ingredient recipe for brewing a sales tonic we have three principles for success in making "cold turkey calls" yield more sales for us:

1. SELL.—Aim to make each "cold turkey call" a selling call. Tackle your prospect with boldness to achieve a surprise. Present something new or present

your product in a different way. Grab your prospect's interest. Be inquisitive. Ask about his needs. Ask about his plans. Show interest in him and in his welfare. This may be flattering to him. It may not. Always anticipate resistance. Overcome it by BOLD SELLING.

2. SERVICE.—Open your eyes to opportunities to serve as well as to sell. Profit by the magic HARD SELL POWER in serving well.

3. CREATE A LOYAL CUSTOMER.—Make the order you write today be the launching pad for writing larger orders tomorrow. Create loyalty among those who buy from you. Give them reasons to believe in you. The salesman's future is secure when he leaves behind him a chain of loyal customers.

Among the experience notes in the records of a number of successful salesmen I found these tips on dealing with doubtful prospects:

(a) If your prospect listens well you're making progress. He's probably sifting. He may be screening. He probably is picking out the kernels that mean something to him from which he thinks he can benefit. Encourage your prospect to talk about his doubts. Then exploit those doubts. Convert them into sales.

(b) The doubtful prospect who admits he is unsure really wants to use what you are selling. What else could cause him to challenge your product? Capitalize on his interest.

(c) The big challenge is to you, not to your prospect. It's up to you to convince your prospect that he will profit or otherwise benefit by taking on what you have to sell. At heart your prospect is a selfish man. Self-interest will get to him. Hammer away at it. DEMONSTRATE, GLAMORIZE, GLORIFY what you have to sell. The triple ingredient HARD SELL TONIC is changing doubters into buyers every day.

Peter Adler got fed up with losing sales to doubters. By BOLD HARD SELL EFFORT he changed the whole picture. He told me that the problem became clear to him when he lost a sale that he was cocksure he had cinched. He realized then that he had actually been afraid of doubters for some time. All the smoke screens he had walked into in his selling career blew in on him again. Now he became fed up. He vowed that he would get rid of fear. He laid out this personal spine-stiffening plan:

(a) He would tackle each prospect with BOLD self-assurance that he could be sold.

(b) He would be on the lookout for ways to serve his prospects better.

(c) He would build up more than a list of customers. He would get an army of loyal customers behind him.

The idea worked for Adler. It can also work for you. Adler doubled his income the first year and his sales are still climbing. He fixed the blame for letting doubters outsell him. He blamed nobody but himself. So he went one step further. He made a daily self-examination a must in his routine. Each night he went over contacts he had made that day. He asked himself a lot of questions, such as these:

AM I SELLING MYSELF to both old and new customers? Am I maintaining a favorable image under fire?

AM I ENTHUSIASTIC? Do I work with enthusiasm? Am I enthusiastic over my product? Do I show enthusiasm for my prospect's business and for his possibilities?

AM I AWAKE TO OPPORTUNITIES to serve my customers and my prospects constructively?

AM I SELF-CONFIDENT or do I appear to be arrogant and arbitrary?

DO I SMILE and show good will when a prospect turns me down?

DO I PLAN AHEAD to make each scheduled call a special call?

AM I AWARE OF THIS TRUISM: "A man frequently digs out of a hole with more enthusiasm than he digs in"?

How to Exploit the Unexpected in Cold Calls
Through Secrets of the Hard Sell

The unexpected may happen to you today. Cold calls especially expose you to the unexpected. You may react in one of two ways: (a) Become confused by the unexpected, or (b) accept the challenge and turn the unexpected development into a sale.

Experienced salesmen, when making "cold turkey" calls, anticipate the unexpected. I heard one "star" salesman tell a group of salesmen one morning about risks that may be involved in dealing with the unexpected. "Crashing a gate to get to a well-fortified prospect is risky," he said, "but, to me, it's worth it. No other excitement is quite like it. Most cold calls I make put me up against new and unexpected obstacles. This sort of resistance wakes me up. It keeps me on my toes. I know of no other tonic that will snap me into line as quickly as a surprise."

Should you encounter the unexpected in making your next "cold turkey" call how do you propose to profit by it? There is no fixed formula for this. But, there are cases which may provide guidelines for you. Honest self-examination comes first. You need to know to what extent you can stand the shock of surprise resistance. You need to know how you will react. You need to know how you propose to deal with the situation.

Salesmen in a wide variety of lines have profited by what I call the "4-I" formula. Each section of the formula begins with the letter "I". This is a formula for personal development. It has been a sales winner for many salesmen. Here, then, is the "4-I" formula. Apply it to yourself. This formula is for exploiting and profiting by the expected in cold calls:

(1) IMAGINATION.—This is the faculty for forming mental images. Creative imagination can solve many of your sales problems. The cold call is a test of your creative ability. Can you imagine any other test that beats it? Put yourself in the position right now of having been turned down in a cold call proposal. Can you imagine how quick action, coupled with creative imagination, might turn that repulse into a closed sale? It has been done. Why not for you?

Specialists tell us that our faculty for creating mental images probably is much keener than we suspect. As the "star" salesman said, breaking down resistance is an exciting, challenging game. It is also profitable. The biggest sales usually are landed after a tussle.

One secret for combating unexpected sales resistance is to keep your imagination alive. Exercise it. One of the specialists referred to declared that arrested development of imagination could be a tragedy for a salesman. Create images. Create images of overcoming the unexpected. Create images of your future sales successes. Creative imagination has been the inception of many of the most amazing sales successes on record.

(2) INGENUITY.—Here we get into the field of planning. Many of our most successful salesmen are image-makers. They are ingenious planners. Ingenuity implies cleverness. It relates to a quick mind. Common sense also gets into the picture. By skillful planning, and by ingenious calculation, great high-rise apartments are replacing squatty dwellings. But, first there was a mental image. Then the idea had to be sold. Evidence of the magic power in the HARD SELL is the changing skyline in a city. Living habits of families are changed. Drabness is overwhelmed by enchantment. Ingenuity, imagination, and the HARD SELL have made it possible. Ingenuity has magic power. It is one of the *Secrets of the Hard Sell*. It multiplies the incomes of salesmen with creative imagination.

(3) INITIATIVE.—Here we have the "get up and go" spirit. Joe Barker's hair-trigger mind quickly grasps the significance in details. Joe detects sales possibilities where other salesmen are blind to these opportunities. Joe is alert. He has a creative mind. He constantly draws mental images. He anticipates the unexpected. Joe does more than smile and rub his hands when he sees a possibility to land a big sale. He understands that he may run into unexpected resistance. . . . But, he has initiative. He acts. He doesn't worry about anticipated resistance. He gets set to meet it and overcome it. He goes after business with HARD SELL VIM. Initiative is a magic force. Joe has cultivated it. Instead of holding back he drives ahead. Initiative has put Joe in the lead. The big sales on his record were landed by initiative fortified by the magic power in *Secrets of the Hard Sell*.

(4) INTEGRITY.—A student in a salesmanship class I attended asked: "Can you sell integrity?" The instructor replied:

"Yes," and for the moment he let it hang there. There is no doubt about it, integrity is basic among the *Secrets of the Hard Sell*. In the long haul, integrity carries a wallop. Because the "cold turkey" call is a door-opener with untold possibilities for future business, integrity can be a sales-builder. As a salesman, you gain status and profit by standing for something. You become known among buyers as "substantial." You become one of their trusted consultants. Your integrity makes those buyers unshakeable prospects, and customers. Integrity has its own magic power among the *Secrets of the Hard Sell*. Ernest L. Wilkinson, a distinguished educator, said: "Whether you succeed or not will depend more upon your integrity than on your brilliance."

To profit by the unexpected requires skill. That is the magic power in the "cold turkey" call. Cold calls test our skills. We learn how to profit by the unexpected. If the unexpected is negative, we turn it around and attack it with positive, persuasive, HARD SELL power. If the unexpected is favorable, we squeeze it to profit by its full potential. We become more and more persistent. We become more and more enthusiastic. We become more and more convincing. We become more and more persuasive. Persistence, enthusiasm, sincerity, and persuasion are all included in the *Secrets of the Hard Sell*.

The representative of one of the nation's outstanding home-study schools spoke to a women's club one night. His subject was artistic talent. After the meeting, a rather shy woman approached him. She believed she had art talent. She was reaching out for encouragement. This was the unexpected in a positive form. She had saved that salesman from making a "cold turkey" call. She then invited him to her home. She showed him her art work. He saw that she did have talent. He launched into a presentation of what professional guidance had done for others. Then came another unexpected development. This time it was negative. "I wish I could do something like that, but I don't see how I can afford it," the woman said. Common sense inspired the salesman to reply: "Can you afford to let your talent die when all you require is an investment of about $1.00 a day? Why, that's even less than a hamburger and a malt at a first class place. You do want to go first class, do you not? Understand, I do not want to push you into this, but I would be less than honest if I didn't tell you that I can see great possibilities in your talent for art. Can you really afford to allow a few cents to hold you back? Why not look over your figures on your income and your expenses once more? See if you can't find just $6 a week for your personal benefit to begin this development program."

The woman found out that it was quite possible for her to pay for the course. Usually this is the case. She enrolled. She completed the course. She won her first public recognition in the state art exhibit. She was on her way. The salesman's judgment, his persuasive selling, and his integrity paid off for him and for the woman. He called on other women to show them how they might become artists. He encouraged some. He enrolled some. But, he also discouraged some. Integrity played a fine role in that salesman's success. He was skillful in handling both positive and negative situations. Even the unexpected.

Why First Calls Rate High on
the Sales Achievement Chart

When you close a first call sale, chalk it up on your personal achievement chart. It's a notable event. Here's why:

You have broken through the ice barrier which is always a first call challenge.

First calls, by their very nature, throw up two-way sales barriers:

(a) Your prospect tightens up. He's thinking: "Uh! Another salesman. How can I get rid of him?"

(b) You feel the chill. You tighten up. You wonder how you can get through to that reluctant prospect.

Your first bid for his favorable attention needs to be warm. A challenging question often does the trick if it suggests to your prospect some sort of reward. Bear in mind, your prospect is vulnerable to his self-interest. He may be cold, stubborn, defiant, and all that, but an appeal to his self-interest will have magic power over those negatives.

Your first test of your HARD SELL influence is how well

you induce him to listen. Then, induce him to talk. When you get your prospect to both listen and talk, sales barriers begin to crumble.

Here's a tip: When your prospect begins to talk don't break in on him. Don't interrupt him. Let him have his say. This is your moment to listen . . . and listen well! Your prospect may have something to say that will unlock the door to a completed sale. What he says may reveal his needs and also his wants. Listen!

All this should happen in the first five minutes of your first interview with a new prospect. If that interview drags out, it loses power. Hopefully, by this time you have loosened up. Hopefully, you have conquered the "first call jitters." Now you should be asking questions. Pertinent questions. All your questions should be directed at drawing your prospect into discussion of your product. Each step should be a persuasive statement or question. It should draw your prospect prominently into the picture.

By this time, you probably have assured your prospect, either directly or by inference, that you are not there to make a hasty buck. You have set him at ease. You may even have told him that you have come to him for information or to get his opinion on uses of what you are selling. Your purpose is to induce him to open up and talk. When he clams up, he's probably cooking up some scheme to ease you out of the door.

When the moment comes for you to talk, speak up. Get to the point. Be direct, Be persuasive. Create mental pictures. Be dynamic. Demonstrate. Speak with authority. Be convincing. *When you make a claim, prove it! Leave nothing in doubt*. Hang on but leave no vital selling points dangling by a thread to haunt you later. Clear up every point as you go along.

First calls on new prospects are the more important calls of your selling day. First calls may be productive or a waste of time. It's largely up to you. To be productive first calls on new prospects may draw upon all the *Secrets of the Hard Sell*. First calls deserve your best sales technique. When you set out to meet your new prospect for the first time be prepared. The following first-call tips may mean dollars in your pocket:

(a) Know your prospect's name.

(b) Know enough about your prospect's business and

about him (or her) to get on favorable speaking
terms.

(c) Call your prospect by name.

(d) Repeat your prospect's name in conversation but
don't overdo it.

(e) Be natural in speech and manners.

(f) Be confident but not overbearing.

(g) Be persuasive. Make your prospect feel that you
consider him (or her) to be the most important
person in the world.

(h) Relate your product to your prospect. Keep both in
the spotlight.

(i) Stimulate discussion but avoid argument.

A newspaper representative I know consistently rates high on
first-call linage sales. In the office, they refer to him as "the ice
breaker." Newspapers in the city were in a HARD SELL competitive battle with TV stations for the advertisers' dollars. When asked
how he set record after record in closing sales against hard competition, that successful salesman replied: "I sell print advertising.
I do not fight the TV tube." The SECRET of that salesman's
achievements in landing new accounts and holding on to established accounts is the HARD SELL. He succeeds by doing a better
selling job than his competitors. He does a better selling job on
"cold turkey" calls. He does a better selling job on subsequent calls.
Instead of waging war on competition, he goes out to secure business. Instead of knocking TV as an advertising medium, he SELLS
print advertising. Simple enough, isn't it? The SECRET is also
simple. It is simply this: There is magic power in the HARD SELL.
Use it to break down resistance. Employ it to close sales.

5

Mastering the Secrets of Hard Sell Word Power

Your most valuable selling tools are words. Choose them well. To hit the high level goals you have set for yourself, release the words that spell out the *Secrets of the Hard Sell*. The record is convincing on how this can be done:

1. Introduce yourself to your prospect with plain, persuasive talk.
2. Make your presentations vibrate with image-creating power produced by HARD SELL words.
3. Use action-inducing words to close your sales.
4. Drive your sales message through to its target with words that bristle with colorful facts and persuasive power.

Not long ago, a group of us were discussing sales problems. One of the men said: "Just talking will get you nowhere. If you hope to sell you've got to say something."

One recognized speech authority contends that plain talk is an art. That seems to be simple enough. Plain talk is made up of words. Until we choose and wisely use the right words, our listeners will fail to "get the picture." We'll just be talking. Until we say something, we are just exercising our vocal muscles. But, by using

HARD SELL WORDS we can say something that will motivate a prospect to buy. We can create wants with HARD SELL words. We can choose words that stimulate desire. We can convince prospects that what we have for sale can benefit them. We can do all this by activating well-chosen HARD SELL WORDS. This is a SECRET OF THE HARD SELL. It builds sales volume.

Blaise Pascal, the French scientist and philosopher, recognized the power of words. In plain talk, Pascal spoke of the impact of words. This is so vital to us as sales people. Pascal pointed to the influence which spoken words have upon our listeners. He said:

"COLD WORDS freeze people . . . . . ."

"HOT WORDS scorch them . . . ."

"BITTER WORDS make them bitter . ."

"WRATHFUL WORDS make them wrathful . ."

Pascal's tribute to word power conceals one SECRET OF THE HARD SELL—which is plain, understandable talk.

Nathaniel Hawthorne had his own ideas about words. As sales people, we can benefit from this thought of Hawthorne's:

"His words had power because they accorded with his thoughts; and his thoughts had reality and depth."

The Hard Sell Principle: Choose well your words! Grasp the power in words. Reinforce your selling power with words. Sell more today than you did yesterday.

To sell Christmas in blazing heat you capitalize on contrasts. Salesmen have been doing this for generations. Many have failed to appreciate the possibilities in exploiting contrasts. Only recently have we found out why contrasts have so much selling power. Contrast becomes persuasive when it has word power behind it.

I recall a blistering hot day when I closed sales by talking about Christmas. I drew the attention of my prospects away from the heat. I was selling printing. It was too hot that day to get far with a prospect by talking about office forms, letterheads, or any other routine matter. Those things were necessary in his business, but winter! That was something else. The contrast got attention in a heat wave. I made my first pitch to a sweltering fuel dealer. A merciless sun was driving business away from him. I saw the sweat on his face. I said nothing about it. Instead I spread out an enticing display of Christmas cards. They were created as business promoters. I had caught his attention. Then I spoke: "This weather puts me in mind of a cold wave that held a grip on this part of the country about a year ago." Suddenly my prospect came to life. "That was one helluva blizzard," he exploded. "All our trucks were running overtime hauling coal. Yes, sir, that was real fuel dealers' weather." It was plain that the thought of Christmas had eased the torture of blistering heat and loss of business. He bought Christmas cards for his business. He also bought Christmas cards for his personal use. It added up to a sizable order for me. All because of a contrast in weather. Getting that business taught me that much selling power is locked up in word power. The thermometer continued to creep up higher but my prospect appeared to be more comfortable. Instead of suffering from heat depression, he was encouraged by my suggestion that snow, ice, Christmas, and fuel dealers' weather were only a few weeks away.

Strange as it may seem, word power can sell Santa Claus even in a heat wave. The SECRET: Capitalize imaginatively on contrast by bold, creative selling. Capitalizing on contrasts is one more SECRET OF THE HARD SELL.

Word power can sell outdoor swimming pools in a blizzard. It can sell more if you tie those words to contrasts. Creativity adds persuasive power to word power even in "impossible" situations. Most lines on the market have untapped possibilities for capitalizing on contrasts. Note the possibilities in the following for working up selling power by hooking HARD SELL words to contrasts:

> Automobiles.—Speedy pickup vs. sluggishness. Gay colors vs. drabness. Rich, thick upholstery vs. cheap, hard-to-clean seat covers. Smooth, quiet engine performance vs. rattling, jarring vibration. Trouble-free, positive action power steering vs. unsafe, uncertain, outdated steering devices.
>
> Wearing apparel.—Radiant, living colors vs. lifeless shades. Creative designing vs. commonplace modeling. Prestige features vs. unimpressive trimmings.
>
> Household heating.—Uniform comfort vs. fluctuating heat with cold spots. Sunshine warmth vs. deep freeze chilliness. Automatic operation vs. manually operated gadgets. Budget plan moderate cost vs. unpredictable operating cost.

THREE SECRETS OF THE HARD SELL in capitalizing on contrasts: (1) Creative prospecting; (2) Creative sales planning; (3) BOLD SELLING.

The creative fuel salesman has a natural alliance with the weather man. When it's hot, he talks about freezing. When it's freezing, he sells warm comfort. Whatever your line may be, search for contrast. Capitalize on contrast. Sell Christmas in blazing heat. Sell healthful, comforting warmth in a blizzard. You can do it with HARD SELL WORD POWER.

Secret Sales-Building Power in
Two-Fisted Hard Sell Words

Let us assume that you are at your prospect's door. All you have to do is reach out, turn the knob and you're in. But, are you going to do the HARD SELL THING when you get in? This is your moment of decision.

When you open the door to a busy prospect's office, it's time for action. Say something or do something that will grab his attention. Arouse his interest. If you delay or fumble you lose ground. While you are fumbling your prospect is sizing you up. Either you capture his interest or he will figure out how to ease you out. But, if you hit that prospect with two-fisted, meaningful words that groove his interest in what you have for sale you're on your way toward making a sale.

In a hard-hitting address, an insurance salesman caught my interest and held it. His talk had depth and substance. He knew what he was talking about. His attitude convinced me of that. For three years that fellow had capped the million dollar goal. He displayed a reverent respect for words. He told us that only by the power of words could we reach the brains of our prospects. "When you are in a man's office," he said, "only words can reach your prospect's mind. And, that same prospect can think only with words."

As sales people, we have recognized that words are our most priceless tools. E. D. Canham, distinguished editor of the *Christian Science Monitor,* once warned about misusing words. "The word is being cheapened," he said. "Everybody talks too much. It is an age of gab. Words are superb tools, priceless instruments. Let us use them well."

How, then, can we use words to sell more? We can show respect for the selling power in words. We can become better acquainted with simple words. Short, simple words repeatedly show their strength as selling tools. For example, take the three-letter word "new." A real estate broker characterizes his major project as a *new* concept in market development. He sells building sites to create a *new* shopping area. He sells those sites to create a *new* mass buying center. He glamorizes the possibilities by flashing *new* ideas for prosperity before his prospects. The key word in his sales pitch is *new*. It has pulling power. Those *new* building sites are selling. There's proof of the power in a short, three-letter word.

A food products manufacturer sends out a special sales force to capitalize on a two-fisted HARD SELL campaign based on this theme: "A *new* idea in ten-minute breakfasts."

A creative, fast-thinking, BOLD SELLING automobile salesman took the direct and positive approach to wrap up his share of business on the day a *new* model was unveiled. His theme: "Here's a *new* development in thrilling car-driving comfort and safety."

A business machine salesman scored favorably with this opening pitch: "In ten minutes of your time I can show you how a revolutionary *new* idea in faster dictation can cut your per letter cost by 18 percent."

A retail shoe salesman developed a prestige clientele. He did this by BOLD SELLING plus judicious use of word-tools. I overheard him make this approach to a banking executive: "Let me slip this shoe on your foot. This is a *new,* scientific idea in shoe construction. Step down, please. Notice the *bedroom slipper comfort* in that shoe? Feel the softness of the leather? Here's the SECRET: It's *all new.* . . . *New* styling. . . . *New* foot protection. . . . *New* wearing quality. . . . *New* all day comfort."

Choice of words is the SECRET in hard-hitting sales talk. HARD SELL WORDS carry the clout necessary to register with your prospect. A choice of dull words can let you down with no sale. As Mr. Canham said: "Words are superb tools. Let us use them well."

On the blackboard in a conference room, in which a real estate sales meeting had just been held, I read this: "It's *little* things that make us *big*." Notice how the contrast of *little* and *big* puts a HARD SELL punch into that seven-word idea. On the floor of that same conference room, I found a slip of paper with these words scribbled on it: "Muscle-bound finances." It's my guess that one of those salesmen in that meeting had a *new* idea on selling and he got it down on paper.

A hardware salesman was a creative fellow. He had HARD SELL ideas and he used HARD SELL WORDS. He did well, too. He sold "cost-cutting" tools. Not just tools. He made ordinary tools "cost-cutting" tools. His sales theme: That a special study had disclosed *new* ways to use tools more effectively to combat rising construction costs. That salesman capitalized on contrasts. He sold an idea. He used HARD SELL WORDS to appeal directly to the pocketbooks of his prospects.

In a HARD SELL campaign, a drug concern used HARD SELL WORDS to put over an idea. In a bold headline on an advertisement for its product, was this 3-word HARD SELL message: "Cool the fever." Note the impact achieved by pitting "cool" against "fever."

Some creative sales-minded person poured a new brand of gin into an ordinary glass bottle of an out-of-the-ordinary shape. This bottle became a talking point for sales representatives. It provided an opportunity for HARD SELL WORDS to get in their persuasive work. The gin people didn't stop with a new bottle. They called on HARD SELL WORDS to complete the selling job. They put a label on the bottle. The gin became more than just dry gin. It became "special dry gin." Three short words for magic HARD SELL POWER.

I overheard a wholesale salesman in a sample room showing of juvenile merchandise. Only once did I hear him refer to "children." He called them "kids." The rather stuffy feminine buyer soon picked up the "kid" idea. "Of course," she said. "We're selling kid stuff aren't we? Why shouldn't we let down our pompous hair and talk about kids?" That salesman got an idea across by frequent use of a three-letter word—kids. He also wrote an order of "sweet" proportions for "kid stuff."

THE HARD SELL PRINCIPLE:—Know and understand your product. Use words that fit the situation. The magic sales-building power in two-fisted words lies in their being specific, never vague.

It Beats all Thunder How the Weather Keeps Up Sales Volume

Of course, thunder is related to weather. We hear the roar of thunder. It awakens us. It's a warning of storm. But, to some salesmen it's a definite challenge. There is excitement connected with thunder. There is also excitement in exceeding yesterday's sales volume by doing a better HARD SELL job today.

When we hook up word power with the weather we come up with a potent concoction that often produces sales. The case of selling Christmas in a heat wave is an example of such potency. Our attitude toward the weather, hot or cold, wet or dry, can have either sales-building power or sales-killing effect.

Mark Twain had a refreshing slant on the weather. A's salesmen we might take these words of his to heart: "The weather is always doing something . . . always attending strictly to business. But it gets through more business in spring than in any other season. In the springtime I have counted 136 different kinds of weather inside of 24 hours."

Mark Twain saw interest in variety of weather. Most of us probably would curse the storm. Where there is so much variety, as Twain pointed out, there could very well be a choice of many *Secrets of the Hard Sell*. By capitalizing on contrasts, such as selling Christmas in a heat wave, we can expand sales volume. Attitude is the key to success.

The HARD SELL SECRET:—A combination of HARD SELL ATTITUDE and HARD SELL WORDS.

Weather has unique sales power. At least it provides us with a conversation topic of common concern. To profit by it all we have to do is convert weather conversation into HARD SELL power by using the magic of HARD SELL words.

For an opener, weather is a natural. You and your prospective buyers are experiencing the same sort of weather today. Both of you also experienced the same weather conditions yesterday. You will also experience similar weather conditions tomorrow. As Mark Twain said, weather is ever-changing. By getting the right attitude toward weather, we can squeeze permanent benefits out of fair weather and foul weather. One thing we can do about the weather is to go right ahead selling our wares. We can refuse to let the thunder scare us away from getting business. With the right attitude toward weather we can cut loose on our prospects with the two-fisted power found in *Secrets of the Hard Sell.*

A stove salesman looked out of his window one morning and saw huge drifts of snow piling up on the land and on the highway. In those parts of the west which he covered, weather often played tricks on merchants and traveling salesmen. On occasions the wind would blow and the snow would drift. Traffic would get snarled. This would keep customers away from stores. It would get salesmen stalled. It was on such a morning that the veteran stove salesman momentarily saw little hope of getting to his dealer-customers. But, this he did know: He had served those customers well. He had won their confidence. He knew their problems. He knew the potential of their market. In some way, he'd get to them and find out how they were making out in the storm. There was a rural telephone line that hooked up to those dealers in that wilderness territory. The stove salesman had an idea that the merchants who often depended on him in tight situations were now praying for stoves. He recalled that he had tried to sell stoves to them in the last heat wave. He couldn't swing the deals at that time. Too hot, they said, to worry about stoves then. But now stove-burning weather had closed in on that territory. The salesman now had dreams of profits for himself if he could get stoves to those merchants. With a "can do" attitude he got busy on the telephone. Yes, sir, those merchants in that snow-bound wilderness wanted stoves and a lot of them. The blizzard and a few well-chosen HARD SELL WORDS did the trick. His supply point assured him that stoves would be on the way by trucks to his waiting merchants. When nightfall came to that isolated area, that salesman had chalked up a heart-warming volume of sales without leaving the comfort of his own fireplace. That salesman had done his homework well. He had sold his customers on himself. He had sold them on his product. When the crisis point arrived, they took him at his word. They bought stoves in volume.

The Hard Sell Principle:—It really does beat all thunder how the weather can keep up sales volume.

A veteran meteorologist once quipped to me: "Weather gets blamed for everything. If you get a cough, it's the weather. If business is bad, it's the weather. If business is good, a change of weather could make it better."

There are salesmen who lean on storm clouds. "I'll wait," some say. "It's too hot to make calls today." Weather is a natural excuse-maker. Not so for a frail young man who sold direct advertising on an exclusive franchise basis. On the opening day of his new line, the weather was bad. His competitor's line also opened on that day. The weather was bad for him, too. But, the young man took off, defying the storm. He closed an exclusive contract with one selected prospect in each town as he passed through. When the score sheets were tallied at sales headquarters, that young salesman topped the list with his opening day sales. His commissions went into the four-figure bracket for the day.

The attitude of that salesman made another case for guts in selling. Flooded highways and heavy storm clouds kept him steamed up instead of defeating him. He was out to sell. With his attitude, it literally did beat all thunder how weather, good or bad, kept up his sales volume the year around.

The Principle:—*Secrets of the Hard Sell,* exposed to all sorts of weather, continue to build sales volume.

Sharpen Your Word Tools to Attain Top Level Hard Sell Impact

The sales girl at the notions counter showed some ordinary lace to a prospective customer. "Isn't this fantastic?" she remarked to the woman. Her "fantastic" remark apparently fell flat. Perhaps we can explain why. Among the many definitions of "fantastic" are these: "Existing only in imagination." "Grotesque." "Eccentric." "Odd." "Incredibly great or extreme." None of these could conceivably have made the lace "fantastic." For this reason, perhaps, use of the word failed to do a "fantastic" selling job.

One SECRET OF THE HARD SELL is to avoid entrapment

by overworked words. Masters of the HARD SELL shun clichés. They use short, meaningful words which have sales-building power.

If you describe your product as "beautiful," or "lovely," or "nice," you miss the full power of HARD SELL WORDS. Such generalities lack vigor. The HARD SELL method is to be specific. What you may consider to be beautiful, or lovely, or nice may not impress your prospect at all. For instance: A flaming sunset grabs you. You see red fingers of fire in the sky. The point is this: The word "flaming" produces an image, more so than "beautiful." For this reason, we sharpen our word tools to give them selling power. We put a keen, HARD SELL edge on words so they can hack through sales barriers. This is another SECRET OF THE HARD SELL. Create persuasive pictures in the mind of your prospect. You can do this with colorful, living words.

For HARD SELL POWER use words that awaken the senses. With such words you can create mental images. You can let your prospect *see* what you mean. You can also use words that suggest that he smell the fragrance of freshly ground coffee. Or point to the electric fan you are selling and say: "Listen to that. It sounds like a whispering breeze."

Salesmen who climb into the five- and six-figure income class have learned to smile at sales resistance. They have drilled themselves to use words with selling power. They make such words their constant companions. They become familiar with their magic.

A simple test has been devised to help you evaluate your ability in selling. With this test you may conceivably pyramid your income as other salesmen have done. This is a self-revealing test. The oftener you repeat the test the more productive it becomes. It's another of the many *Secrets of the Hard Sell*.

With the magic of words you can step out today with renewed HARD SELL POWER. You can do this by enthusiastically testing yourself. The following test is set up as a daily exercise in sharpening your word tools. Fifteen minutes a day have expanded the HARD SELL vocabularies of other salesmen. They have increased their income. They can do the same for you. Here's how:

Read the following objections. They seem familiar to you, don't they? They are familiar to most salesmen. But, now to the test! Choose HARD SELL WORDS to rebut each of the following commonplace objections. Reach for words that can stand up and convert these ten objections into sales:

1. Your price is too high. It's out of line.
2. I can't afford to buy now. See me later.
3. I'll have to talk this over with my partner.
4. I'm too busy to go into this today. See me on your next trip.
5. There's no demand here for your product.
6. I think I'd better shop around.
7. I don't believe in insurance. I'm over-insured now.
8. Let me think this over for a while.
9. I understand this car is a real gas hog.
10. Why advertise? We have more business now than we can handle.

The Hard Sell Principle:—"Bright is the ring of words when the right man rings them."—*Robert Louis Stevenson.*

Choose Simple Words to Clarify and to Sell with Secrets of the Hard Sell

You're in! You have been admitted to a prospect's office. You have been told that this man is hard-boiled. Quickly you make this estimate of the situation and plan your action:

(a) You'll bet this man puts a cash value on minutes. You decide to waste no time sparring with this guy.

(b) You decide to hit him with crisp, understandable proposals, rich in self-interest appeal.

(c) You move to get your prospect involved in the sales process. With pertinent questions you reach out to draw him into the picture. You'll strive to keep up a dialogue with this tough guy. You'll be positive in your own statements. Your prospect's interest must be maintained. You'll make him and his use of your product the center of interest. You'll seek his opinion on profitable ways of using your product. This flatters him. You have put him on a pedestal. You have recognized him as an expert. Again and again you'll draw on his reservoir of knowledge. You'll ask him for his opinions and also for his recommendations on profitable uses of your product.

(d) Now you are moving steadily toward the close. The magic of your HARD SELL WORDS is taking effect. Your prospect is responding favorably. You have nearly completed filling out the order blank which has been in plain sight during the entire dialogue. You ask your prospect if 2,000 will be enough as a trial order. He meditates. You suggest again, "Perhaps 2,500 would be more like it." He agrees. The deal is closed by liberal use of *Secrets of the Hard Sell.*

The simple word is the key to grabbing and holding a prospect's interest. Forget about long, fancy words. Put your faith in short, meaningful words. Hang on to your prospect's interest. Never be dull. Keep your presentations alive. Use words of action. They're the HARDEST SELLING WORDS. They keep interest at high pitch if they're tied to the self-interest of your prospect.

To give your prospect a clear picture, you try to get a firm grip on his undivided attention. You may even tell him why it is so important to him that he give you his undivided attention. Make this a crucial moment. Cause him to believe that he may be missing something if he doesn't listen.

At each step in your presentation, make it appear that your call on him is vital to his welfare. Again, if necessary, tell him so. The act of telling your prospect may intensify his interest. He begins to wonder why this is so all-fired important to him. He may even ask you why. And, you tell him with greater power in your HARD SELL WORDS.

Check the following five steps for a productive interview with a prospect. (This is another revealing self-interest test. It involves another SECRET OF THE HARD SELL.) It's to your self-interest to find out how you stack up in this highly competitive race for business. Here are the five steps:

Step No. 1—Take a good look at yourself. Clean shaven? Hair trimmed? Shoes polished? Clothes conservative and neat? (If you're selling a luxury product or a prestige item, measure up to expectations. Look the part.)

Step No. 2—Move in with confidence. Make this a smiling eye-ball to eye-ball contact. Be natural. Be sure of yourself. Not cocky. Be cool. Anything can happen. Make your introduction in simple, moving words. Make this a call of high level importance to your prospect. Do this with the greatest possible economy of words. For this step, mobilize short, colorful, active HARD SELL WORDS.

Step No. 3—With hard-hitting words develop your theme. Clarify and reclarify all points that pertain to benefits for your prospect. Be sure that you are sold on what you are trying to sell to him. As a self-test, turn those HARD SELL WORDS on yourself. Keep the dialogue with your prospect running. This is a battle to be won or lost by words.

Step No. 4—Tighten up weak links in your sales talk. Take no chances. Clarify and reclarify by frequent recapitulation. Tell and retell are two vital SECRETS OF THE HARD SELL. Both challenge your command of HARD SELL WORD POWER. Now you are heading for the pay-off point. Closing time is crowding up on you!

Step No. 5—The close! Use HARD SELL WORDS with showmanship to induce your prospect to decide and act favorably on your presentation. By this time, you should have asked your prospect for the order at least three times and in at least three distinctive ways. By this time, your prospect should be accustomed to seeing your order book. (You should have had it before him since Step No. 2.) If you have done this, you will not risk losing the self-interest grip on your prospect while you fumble to find your order book. At this point, press gently, but firmly, for a buying commitment. Be prepared to convert any delaying action on his part into HARD SELL reasons for buying now. All this focuses the spotlight on the magic power of words. A simple 3-point formula for closing a sale is this:

1. Clarify and reclarify with simple, understandable words.

2. Keep the dialogue running. Stimulate it with short interesting words.

3. Close with active words. Close with impressive words. Close with short, simple HARD SELL WORDS that are saturated with their own SECRET POWER. Ask for the order!

Public speaking and salesmanship are closely related. In each the key is command of persuasive words. In salesmanship the objective is to persuade, to convince, then to promote buying action. In public speaking the objective is similar. The skillful speaker aims at the heart of his listeners. He draws them into his persuasive net. He induces them to believe as he believes. He inspires them to act as he wants them to act.

The salesman and the public speaker profit by using the same tools. Word tools are their chosen instruments. With both of them, HARD SELL WORDS are the most effective in hurtling over and through barriers.

Ten points chart the course of masters of the HARD SELL. These ten points are the keys to successful presentations. Observe how skillfully these points are used by dynamic public speakers and by top producing salesmen. In your observation, become conscious of how you can profit by these ten points in making your manner of expression more persuasive. In doing this, avoid making these points immovable fixations. Avoid becoming stilted in speaking. Let your hair down. Loosen up. Speak as though you really mean it! Speak out as though you sincerely believe it!

Here, then, are those ten SECRETS OF THE HARD SELL. Here are ten tested suggestions for putting magic power into your sales presentations:

1. Converse. Don't preach.
2. Speak out! Don't mumble!
3. Use plain words. Skip the fancy words.
4. Favor nouns and verbs. Go easy on adjectives and adverbs.

5. Scratch the long word if a short word will do the job.
6. Be positive. Not negative.
7. Cut it short. Going on and on with vague objectives is deadening.
8. Be yourself. Imitations lack selling power.
9. Create mental images with "picture" nouns.
10. Stimulate desire to buy with action verbs.

Most of the high producing salesmen I have known are, in fact, artists. They paint pictures with words. They create images in the minds of their prospects. We can jack up our production by speaking clearly, with sincerity, and by utilizing the magic power in HARD SELL words. This is the dollar-making purpose of letting words fall from our lips in the market place.

Sir Joshua Reynolds once pointed out the persuasive power in simplicity. His was an artist's viewpoint. He painted pictures with a brush. We, as salesmen, attempt to "paint" pictures with words. We, too, can profit by the persuasive power in simplicity. Reynolds, a noted artist, said: "Simplicity is an exact medium between too little and too much." This, too, is a SECRET OF THE HARD SELL.

Paint Tempting Hard Sell Pictures with the Magic Power in the Color of Words

J. K. (Jim) Kanzler is a HARD SELL salesman. I have seen his record. I have seen him in action. He handles words as an artist would handle a brush. When Jim talks, he is painting word pictures. To create images in the minds of his prospects, he combines persuasive ideas with simple words. I can visualize Jim now. He's about to tackle a prospect. He's a busy man as he enters his prospect's office. His own hot idea has him steamed up. His prospect seems to catch the fever as Jim goes into action. Jim's enthusiasm radiates light on his idea. Even stiff sales resistance makes him smile. His unruffled control of the situation seems to impress his prospect. Jim continues to bore in. He speaks with enthusiasm. At a moment of his own choosing he cuts in with this question: "Get the picture?" Jim may get a nod of agreement or he may get a brusque, "No, I don't get the picture!" In either case, Jim has succeeded in clearing the way for "painting" more tempting pictures with the magic power in the color of words.

Jim now moves in with steady persuasive force. He begins by "painting" a picture of leisurely comfort in a hillside home, which he is selling. He backs up his HARD SELL words with enticing photographs. He points out the unobstructed view from the home he is trying to sell. He describes "flaming sunsets" seen from that vantage point. He tells his prospect how Mrs. Gardner has turned a similar home site into a prize-winning flower bed of snow-white, autumn-yellow and blood-red roses. Jim goes on sketching a word picture of personal security in that home for his prospect. For a moment he dwells on the sturdy construction of the home. He describes the sweet smell of the forest near that home site. "That house is a monument to the green-forested mountain from which much of the building material in that house came," he tells his prospect. "In that quiet setting you can hear the trickle of cool, clear water bubbling out of a mountain spring. You will hear the chirp of birds. You will see squirrels skipping across your door yard. It's a wonderland of peace. You'll find it to be a relaxing paradise in all seasons."

Note the following HARD SELL, image-creating words Jim used in his sales presentation:

Leisurely comfort.	Sturdy timber.
Hillside home.	Green-forested mountain.
Unobstructed view.	Trickle of cool, clear water.
Flaming sunset.	Bubbling spring.
Prize-winning garden.	Chirp of birds.
Snow-white roses.	Squirrels skipping.
Autumn-yellow roses.	Wonderland of peace.
Blood-red roses.	Relaxing paradise.

Jim was building his prospect up to drive out for a look at the real thing. He had been selling from photographs. Now it was time to capitalize on the word-picture he had created.

Not long ago, Jim discovered the magic power in words. He put this power to work for him. He is now closing sales that had seemed "impossible" before. He has stepped up from the ordinary class and has entered the $28,000 and up income class.

You, too, can choose words that have the magic power to create HARD SELL images in the minds of your prospects. Here are ten tips for making stimulating HARD SELL presentations with word-magic:

1. Use simple, image-creating words. Glorify your product. Suppress the temptation to exaggerate. Instead, paint a factual, colorful, desirable, believable picture.

2. Use words that dig into the emotions. Appeal to the heart.

3. Use image-creating words. Strive to develop in your prospects an irresistible desire to possess what you have for sale.

4. Use persuasive words that pull on the selfish nature of man.

5. Use HARD SELL words that create images of success.

6. Use image-creating words that tickle the vanity.

7. Use image-creating words that capitalize on envy.

8. Use HARD SELL words that stimulate images of profit-making.

9. With HARD SELL words picture your product as a way to greater security for your prospects.

10. Capitalize on the desire for luxury and leisure by using image-creating HARD SELL words.

The Hard Sell Principle:—Bold selling is closely linked to image-making. The key to success in the HARD SELL is to THINK BIG.

Successful salesmen are economical in their use of words. They are discriminating. They have learned that the short, descriptive word has HARD SELL power. They have also learned that a torrent of words rarely produces torrential selling power. As Alexander Pope once wrote: "Words are like leaves and where they most abound, much fruit of sense beneath is seldom found."

"Get the picture?"

6

Landing the Tough Ones with the Secrets of Hard Sell Timing

Even the toughest of the tough ones wilt and buy when the magic of good timing gets to them.

The secret of good timing lies in knowing your prospects. To know your prospect well enough to bring him to a decision favorable to you requires that you know the answers to the following two questions:

1. HOW DOES HE WORK?
2. WHAT MAKES HIM TICK?

Habit plays a big part in your prospect's working methods. Take a look at yourself. Doesn't habit play a part in how you work? Well, habit also has a grip on your prospect. You can bet on that. He may be a tough nut to crack. Or, he may be wide open for any sort of sales pitch. In either case, he is, to some extent, a creature of habit. He has pet ways of doing his thing. Find out all about his pet ways. Find out what his thing is. Study him. Understand him. Learn how he has become what you now consider him to be—a "live," desirable prospect. Time your approach to fit into his pet ways of doing things. Get on favorable ground with him. This requires good timing. The elementary secret of good timing is this: *Tackle your prospect at a favorable moment, not when he is swamped with other problems.*

In Chapter 2 we gained a fresh insight into HARD SELL TIME MANAGEMENT. That related specifically to us. It related to how we can most profitably handle the minutes and hours allotted to us. It related to the productive use of precious minutes and hours. Now we are being exposed to another side of the time problem. We call it "timing." This is related to time management but only to this extent: The magic of timing relates specifically to *how* to become more sensitive to proper timing. Doing this you can beef up your minutes and hours with HARD SELL POWER. For instance:

An insurance salesman I know times many of his sales calls to reach newlyweds. He times other calls to reach parents soon after the arrival of a new-born baby. He times other calls to reach those bereaved by death. He brings to these saddened prospects a timely message of how insurance protection can take the financial sting out of death. This same salesman times other calls to boost his sales. He reaches out to recent buyers of homes. He zeros in on a prospect who has just stepped up into the executive class.

The GOLDEN SECRET OF THE HARD SELL is the magic of timing. Incorporated in this golden secret are two related secrets:

1. THE "NOW" SECRET.—The magic of good timing.
2. THE "GO" SECRET.—The magic of decisive action.

The secret of successful timing is in SEEING, in FEELING, in DECIDING and in unhesitatingly going into hard sell action. The secret of hard sell timing is the knack of choosing the right moment to talk, the right moment to remain silent, the right moment to press for action. The secret of successful timing is the HARD SELL SKILL of knowing when and how to act.

When your prospect reflects a mood of anxious interest in what you have to sell you can be reasonably sure you have touched the magic cord of timing. Be sensitive to such reactions. Be sensitive to moods. Be sensitive to attitudes and to responses. In all of them there is TIMING SIGNIFICANCE.

In timing your sales calls be aware of these four HARD SELL FACTS:

1. There are early-morning buyers.
2. There are mid-day buyers.
3. There are afternoon buyers.
4. There are nighttime buyers.

Many big ticket prospects prefer the shadows of the evening. They prefer to get into the ramifications of taking on something new or involved in the uninterrupted quiet of the night. The secret of activating the magic of timing is finding out the moment most favorable for influencing each prospective buyer on your list.

To find out what makes your prospect tick, do some serious in-depth re-evaluation of him. This pays high dividends. For example, an insurance counselor who had his million score in sight called this sort of re-evaluation his "prospecting encore." That salesman detailed to me how he profited by taking special note of a prospect. He noted that the prospect was a "bundle of nerves." To that salesman his prospect's nervousness had both timing and sales significance. Why? Because, as he said, "it was a warning to tread lightly. A jittery prospect requires patient, special treatment. Only by such treatment can you pull him away from being just a prospect and change him into a buyer." The counselor suggested that every salesman take note of a prospect who obviously makes special effort to appear calm and pleasant. "Perhaps his persistent smile is a cover-up. Perhaps his smile hides a fire-cracker temper. If this is the case that prospect can be easily touched off and a sale can be killed. That prospect requires a special kind of HARD SELL diplomacy to convince him that he should buy and to retain that smile on his face."

I learned from that successful HARD SELL insurance counselor that he also did certain things in timing which you and I can do and profit by them. Here are some of the sales-producing steps he suggested:

1. Find out the ideal time of day (or night) to talk business with your prospect.

2. Learn if your prospect is an early-morning, high-gear starter. This you can find out through observation, through conversation, through *Secrets of the Hard Sell* which stimulate your prospect to open up and talk about himself. When he opens up, LISTEN!

3. Learn if your prospect is the quick clean-up type. Does he work at a cluttered desk? Or, is his desk usually orderly? Does he get details out of the way early in the day? Could this possibly be to make time for him to meditate, to plan, or even to make time to hear a salesman out?

4. Is your prospect a speed-thinker or a plodder? Find out. Gauge the tempo of your sales presentation to conform to the temper of your prospect.

In most sales successes, the magic of timing is involved. The magic of timing is the GOLDEN SECRET OF THE HARD SELL. If your prospect is a night owl, why risk the loss of business by going after him at dawn? Why not recognize what you are up against and make the most of it? Why cut down your odds of success by tackling the night owl at an hour when the pressure pile on his desk demands his immediate attention? The profitable way is to ride with the current. Glide into the tempo of your prospect for easier, more productive HARD SELL results.

Time is your stock in trade in the HARD SELL. You have at your disposal the right time and the wrong time. The magic of timing lies in choosing the right time. This is one SECRET OF THE HARD SELL that lands the tough ones.

How to Detect Timing Signals for Turning On the Magic Power of the Hard Sell

Whoever dreamed of a lame man being a timing signal for selling? Well, it happened, in the lobby of an office building. A salesman waiting for an elevator spotted an executive he had previously met. The man was limping. This alerted the salesman. It was his timing signal. He carried a line of "foot comfort" shoes. In due time he entered that executive's office with samples of his shoes. He showed the limping man shoes that would make walking a pleasure. Shoes that had class. Shoes made of soft, durable, tough leather. That salesman's shoes were packed with foot comfort qualities. He made it appear that they were. The signal that gave that salesman his opening was a lame man. It was the "go" signal for him. It touched off his HARD SELL magic. The result: (a) A sale; (b) Repeat sales.

If you are on the alert you'll see timing signals pop up in the most unusual places. They'll show up at unexpected times. HARD SELL salesmen profit by quickly seizing upon such signals. As Agesilaus, a King of Sparta, put it centuries ago: "It is circumstance and proper timing that give an action its character and make it either good or bad."

In my breaking-in days in selling, first calls "bugged" me. First calls were less productive for me than other calls. This gave me some encouragement. It seemed to tell me that I could sell if I hung on. I did some serious self-examination. I found out why my first calls fell flat. This is what I discovered: I enjoyed meeting people. I enjoyed "gab" sessions with prospects. I felt good when I came out of those sessions. Then the cold reality of what I was doing came clear to me. I was doing a swell job of hand-shaking but I was coming out empty-handed. Nobody needed to tell me that hand-shaking alone wouldn't feed my kids. I had to do more selling and less visiting. As I progressed in the business, I also learned that to build volume I had to do HARD SELLING. The milk-toast sales pitch didn't do the job. I came to the conclusion that I would have to do an about-face. I concluded that my mission as a salesman was not entirely a public relations venture. It had to be spiced with HARD SELL magic if I was going to close sales. At that point I began to watch more closely for timing signals. I saw them as I walked along the street. I began to see those timing signals while I was interviewing prospects. A prospect's flash of interest became a signal for me to turn on the HARD SELL. A problem which might irk my prospect became a timing signal. It revealed his interest. I found that this often was the high buying point.

A remark by a prospect to his secretary once led me to a substantial sale. As I entered that prospect's office, he was saying to his secretary: "We'll have to make a decision on those invitations for our remodeling sale and open house." I sold printing. That prospect had dropped a timing signal for me. I picked it up and wrapped up a satisfactory order for a first call. This broke the ice for me. That man became a regular buyer. The account grew in volume as I continued to call on him with new ideas.

You can build sales volume, as others have done, by catching the timing principle in the following Biblical phrase: "A time to get, and a time to lose; a time to keep and a time to cast away."—Eccl. 3:6. That passage points up the necessity and the importance to us of detecting timing signals, for "to everything there is a season, and a time to every purpose under heaven."—Eccl. 3:1.

An energetic salesman who sold uniforms direct to industrial and business concerns and to institutions had driven past a certain bakery every morning for months. One morning a timing signal rang a bell in his brain. That morning he saw what he had seen before—driver-salesmen assembling at the plant. He wondered if there was a pep rally every morning. He had a hunch that this might be a good time to crash the gate. Both management and the driver-salesmen might be in the mood to put some advertising power into their uniforms. He played his hunch. In this HARD SELL, first-call presentation, he closed a substantial sale and kept the door open for doing regular business with that firm.

A mobile-home dealer who was aiming high for sales volume observed the impatience of one of his salesmen. The man was showing a middle-aged couple the homes on display. Then a younger, more attractive couple came on the lot. He gave up the older couple, leaving them to wander and look. The dealer noticed that the old couple returned again and again to a large home on the lot. This was his timing signal to take action. He got the older couple excited about the refinements in that one display home. They talked about how nice it would be to have such luxurious living quarters as they shifted from place to place on their large ranch during the planting and harvest seasons. This was the only display home in which the dealer had placed a portable radio. It was turned on, playing soft music. During the closing action the rancher's wife asked: "Does the radio go with the home?" The dealer-salesman smiled and replied: "To you, yes. Even two radios, one for each of you, free, if you wish." The magic of timing had done its job and an $8,000 sale had been made to the tune of a "free radio."

There was a lesson in that sale for other salesmen. The salesman who gave up and made no sale that day failed to detect timing signals which came clear to his employer. He had drawn "live" prospects away from the mobile home that had been the first to attract their attention and interest. He had ignored the persuasive power of a bit of background music in that one mobile home. He failed to capitalize on it. He underestimated the purchasing power of the well-heeled older couple. He later admitted that the rancher's coveralls had misled him. He had sized up the younger couple as newlyweds, which they were. But, when the showdown came, they lacked the wherewithal to buy a mobile home.

The salesman-dealer scored higher than his employed salesman that day because he capitalized on good timing. He capitalized on timing signals. He capitalized on the magic power in *Secrets of the Hard Sell.*

How to Create a Favorable Hard Sell Climate by Altering Your Timing

One of the *Secrets of the Hard Sell* is the art of compromise. This is an art frequently overlooked. In salesmanship, compromise amounts to creating a situation in which both the buyer and the seller can live together and prosper. For instance:

Prospect "A" is holding out for a price concession. He wants a discount. He wants a "better deal."

Salesman "B," bound by house rules, cannot be a price-cutter to get business. He must sell! Thus the problem becomes personal with him. He must find a way to compromise. He must either persuade Prospect "A" to soften or Salesman "B" must alter his timing to create a more favorable HARD SELL CLIMATE. Salesman "B" chooses the latter course. He succeeds in this way:

> (a) He shifts away from price discussion. He concentrates on exclusive features of his product. He induces Prospect "A" to discuss quality and the profit

motive in handling quality goods. This becomes a high level appeal. It is a challenge in HARD SELL PERSUASION.

(b) He asks Prospect "A" how he managed to develop his notable sales volume on quality merchandise.

(c) By that question, Salesman "B" involves Prospect "A" in the selling process. In answering Salesman "B's" question, Prospect "A" commits himself to some extent. Salesman "B" now steers still farther away from the price tag.

(d) Salesman "B" alters his timing and also his approach. He bids for approval of the quality value of what he has to sell. Already Prospect "A" has expressed his favor for quality. Salesman "B" takes it from there, continuing to side-step price.

(e) Salesman "B" is now setting his timing for the closing moment. He tightens his sales presentation. Step by step he hammers away on the sales and profit potential in his quality product. Thus Salesman "B" creates a favorable HARD SELL CLIMATE in which both Salesman "B" and Prospect "A" can live, progress, and prosper.

Salesman "B" achieves his objective in these five steps:

1. By skillful, HARD SELL TIMING.

2. By altering his timing to break through the price barrier.

3. By capitalizing on a more favorable sales climate which he has created.

4. By timing each step in his sales presentation to achieve maximum HARD SELL POWER.

5. By altering his timing whenever and wherever necessary.

The key to altering the timing of Salesman "B's" presentation was found when Prospect "A" made his strong bid for price concession. In doing that, Prospect "A" disclosed that he was, indeed, "sold" on what Salesman "B" had for sale. He was now haggling for price. To Salesman "B" this was a timing signal. At that point, Salesman "B" profited by altering his timing. Quickly he swung away from price. He pounded on quality and the benefits in quality for Prospect "A". Already Prospect "A" had given his endorsement of the profit value in quality.

In another case, a creative salesman ran into a solid sales barrier. It happened this way: He made the error of assuming that an established customer was going to buy again. He was leaning on writing an order rather than making a sale. That salesman represented an exclusive calendar and advertising specialty house. His account was a bank. The bank had used that salesman's calendars for years. On this trip, the salesman found a new advertising executive in the saddle at the bank. This should have been a signal to that salesman, but he failed to respond to it. Consequently, his approach to the new executive was off key. He assumed that the new executive was going to follow in the footsteps of his predecessor. This, however, was not the case. Nor did the salesman's assumption swell the ego of the new executive. Fortunately, the salesman realized that he had createl a bad climate for selling. By a quick shift in his timing and a quick revision of his approach, he squeezed out of his predicament. Moreover, he sold that new executive advertising specialties in such quantity that the total of his order far exceeded the usual expenditure for calendars.

Effective communication is the key to creating a favorable HARD SELL climate. We can alter our timing and thereby establish more favorable communication. By accomplishing this we improve our sense of timing. We see the profitable results of timing.

Edmund Burke, the distinguished English statesman, once said: "Every human benefit and enjoyment . . . is founded on compromise and barter." Therein we see more clearly the significance of improving communication. We see the HARD SELL NEED for being more responsive to timing and to timing signals. We compromise to get on firm ground with our prospects. We barter with them. We persuade them to pay our price for what we have to sell. By the magic power in the HARD SELL we have stimulated a desire to buy. We have become flexible in our bartering. We have improved the HARD SELL CLIMATE. We have altered our timing wherever this has become desirable, profitable, or otherwise favorable to us. This has been done with a HARD SELL compromising attitude.

Flexibility is the key to profiting by stern resistance. It is directly related to the art of HARD SELL persuasion. We compromise only to achieve our ends. THE SECRET? Here it is: To maintain sales momentum against all obstacles. To maintain HARD SELL enthusiasm. To maintain HARD SELL persistence. To take advantage of all TIMING SIGNALS. To conquer tough situations and land the tough ones by the MAGIC OF TIMING.

Three Tested Timing Rules for Cracking the Shells of Hard-to-Sell Prospects

Some hard-to-sell buyers boast of the number of salesmen they turn away empty-handed. One robust character I knew had the reputation of being hard to get. We lunched together when I came to his town. One story he told was about how he "cooled" a salesman who had tackled him without preparing for the fray. My tough friend laughed about this incident. He chuckled about other similar incidents. But, I recall my first sale to that fellow. Looking back at that break-through, it doesn't seem that it was too difficult. It only involved adequate preparation. It also involved time and a few other HARD SELL ploys. Well, he gave me his power play. Right off I recognized that he was bent on deflating me. But, what he probably did not realize was that I was getting someting of value from each thrust he made at me. In those thrusts I detected something commendable. I complimented him for what he said and what he did. This pleased him. Like most tough guys he smacked his lips when I flattered him. When I said something good about him, his fire began to go out. He became tractable. I continued to sell to that man in succeeding years. My success with him probably was due to the fact that I never tried to push him. At least, not obviously. I led him like a balky horse right up to the watering trough. Even then, I couldn't force him to drink. He wasn't the type to be forced to do anything against his will. With a man such as he was I had to have some sense of timing. I constantly watched for opportunities to compliment him. I always thanked him when he signed an order and then I complimented him for the wisdom of his decision to buy. You see, I thereby made the sale his decision, not mine. Timing was the secret. I sustained our friendship through the years by good timing. Timing became the magic power in the HARD SELL persuasion which changed this "tough one" from a hard-to-sell prospect to a satisfied, profitable customer.

Three fundamental rules are involved in timing that produces sales. First there is total preparation to overcome sales resistance. Next comes self-confidence. And, third, closing by skillful timing.

Try to recall your last selling problem. How did you handle it? How did you come out? Now check that problem and how you handled it with three fundamental rules. Next time you have an appointment to go up against a "hard-to-sell" prospect, go over the following three rules before you keep that appointment:

(1) PREPARE!—What do you really know about your prospect? Do you know enough about him for you to sell to this man who is touted as a "tough guy"? Remember, you are taking him on in his own arena. He has that advantage over you. Prepare yourself to overcome that barrier. Strengthen yourself with abundant knowledge of your product and its uses. Know all you can find out in advance about your prospect, about his reputation, about his method of operation. Learn how he succeeds and why he fails. Know enough about that "tough guy's" business to talk convincingly with him. Such knowledge will give you self-confidence. Tough guys seem to enjoy picking on timid sales people. Don't run scared. Prepare yourself to crack the shell of tough sales resistance. *Secrets of the Hard Sell,* which include TIMING, contain that magic power which gets through to the hearts of hard-to-sell prospects.

(2) COURAGE DOES IT!—Move in on your hard-to-sell prospect with sureness of victory. He admires vigor. He may never admit it, but positive, firm sureness reduces his fire. It causes him to think. When you see this change of pace in your prospect, it's your timing signal. It's time to strike at your prospect's most vulnerable points.

> (a) Appeal to your tough prospect's needs (predetermined by your careful preparation to tackle this prospect). Show him how easy it can be for him to enjoy and profit by getting those needs which you have for sale.

(b) Determine his wants. Lead him into revealing commitments. Involve him in the selling process. The more he talks, the more revealing he'll become. When he indicates he has a desire for something, try to fit your product into his wants.

The art of timing plays a big part in the foregoing steps. It's all fuel for the power-thrust which breaks down stubborn sales resistance. It's all included in the *Secrets of the Hard Sell.*

(3) CLOSE AT THE HIGH POINT!—This is your zero hour. Now comes the final thrust. This may come sooner than you had anticipated. By skillful timing, your presentation has caught your prospect at his low resistance point. You have been using HARD SELL TECHNIQUES all the way. You have timed each step to blend with the selling climate. You have taken note of your prospect's reactions. You have seen his interests mount. You have picked up the time signals and you have capitalized on them. Now it's time to close!

Your major sales thrust has been reserved for this pay-off moment. Your closing action has been timed to meet the demands of this high point in your prospect's interest. He's "hot." He is responding well. He sees how what you have to sell is related to his needs. He sees how it relates to his wants, his plans.

You have detected each TIMING SIGNAL your prospect has given you. Or, you should have done so. THE RESULT: Another sale closed through the magic power in *Secrets of the Hard Sell.* Another shell of sales resistance cracked by skillful timing. Another shell of sales resistance cracked by persuasive power to stimulate buying action.

How to Change Horses in Midstream by Hard Sell Timing to Prevent Business from Slipping Away

When you feel business slipping out of your fingers the HARD SELL THING TO DO is to find out *why?* Then act!

Your master sales plan may be too rigid. You may not be flexible enough. You may rely too heavily on the old ways. You may exclude new ideas. You may be too complacent. You may be blind to TIMING SIGNALS. Hard-to-sell prospects frequently flash those signals to you.

When you feel business slipping away from you, consider changing horses, even in midstream. To make such a change you need to rely on HARD SELL TIMING.

Perhaps you have had this experience or something similar to it:

You have prepared well to make a sales presentation to a prospect whom you have carefully selected from your list of customers. In choosing this prospect you feel that you have one advantage—your previous sales to him. This time, however, you have a new product. This merits consideration. You plan a fresh approach. You give it a new "twist." No longer is your customer just a customer. At this stage you have made him a prime prospect. So you warm up to release on him the magic power of the HARD SELL. In all of your planning for this sales venture, you have had in mind many of the *Secrets of the Hard Sell*. You are aware that to sell this new idea to this established customer presents a major challenge. Routine selling (order taking) won't do the job. Therefore, you plunge into the mainstream with your presentation. Soon you detect that your timing is bad. Your prospect has gone cold on you. What to do? You call up your reserve strength. At this point you need the strength of two qualifications:

1. FLEXIBILITY.—The ability to bend with the wind. The ability to float with the tide.

2. RESOURCEFULNESS.—The power to call up reserve strength. That power is dependent on how well you have stocked your arsenal with new creative ideas.

Do you possess such qualifications?

One SECRET OF THE HARD SELL is to make quick adjustment to unforeseen developments in any sales situation.

Do you bend with the wind when the sales wind blows against you? Or, do you try to fight the hurricane? *Secrets of the Hard Sell* contain the principles which enable you to cope with any surprise rebuffs.

How resourceful are you? New ideas held in reserve to be presented in new and challenging situations can provide you with a new slant on HARD SELL MAGIC.

New ways for your prospect to profit or otherwise benefit by buying from you contain the magic power of the HARD SELL.

Being ready and qualified to "change horses in midstream" endows you with that magic power which shoots sales volume upward in spite of unforeseen obstacles.

These principles in *Secrets of the Hard Sell* may appear to be inconsistent with what has been your sales strategy. In the HARD SELL there is often magic power, even in inconsistency. George W. Romney, who was rated as a better-than-average salesman, had this thought on inconsistency:

"There is no virtue in what we call 'consistency' as it is usually understood. Flexibility—the willingness to change with changing conditions—is essential in this dynamic and progressive world."

Selling securities in volume was the overpowering ambition of a steady producer who came to my attention. This man was constantly looking for tomorrow's opportunities. He was never totally satisfied with today's accomplishments. He also said he had never been able to come up with an idea that had the power to influence every prospect in the same way. This challenged him. "I have sold stocks totaling millions," he said. "In virtually every sale, large or small, I have had to be flexible. I have had to be resourceful. If I had not been able to sell against an adverse change of the wind I would never have succeeded in this business. Call it hard sell, soft sell, or luck, as you choose, the end result is all that really matters. I have found no substitute for hard selling to build up a solid sales growth. To reach the closing point of a sale, I have had to change my direction several times. I think that requires a combination of resourcefulness and flexibility."

A book salesman was pushing sales upward on a "home library" theme. He spent an evening by appointment with a family which included the parents, a young son, and a young daughter. In age, the son and daughter were only two years apart. The salesman opened with a strong boy-interest idea. Getting the parents involved in the selling process tipped off the salesman that neither the son nor the daughter had brought home much glory in their school grades. The salesman detected vague timing signals which told him to make his thrust at the father and not at the boy. To do this he became aware that he would have to "change horses in midstream." But he was a flexible, resourceful man. He caught the father's interest quickly. He opened one of the volumes and showed the father how he could have at his finger tips a rich source of knowledge by which he could help that boy to get over his hurdles at school. This appealed to the father. The salesman hammered away to build up the father's pride in himself and also in his boy.

The mother overheard all this and she contracted the book fever. She wanted to do something constructive and helpful for her daughter. By HARD SELL TIMING, by flexibility, by resourcefulness that salesman was on his way to wrapping up a substantial sale. He had capitalized on many angles included in the *Secrets of the Hard Sell*. The kids were pleased with the outcome. They were eager to get that "home library." With their parents so eager to become teachers, the boy and the girl hoped they had found an escape route through which they could cut down on studying. As they saw it, their parents could do both the studying and teaching. This appealed to them and the book fever was contagious. Pa, ma, and the kids bought the idea.

In this sales venture, the magic power of TIMING was vital. This is what happened:

The salesman capitalized on the right moment to nourish the ego of the father.

The salesman capitalized on the right moment to detect that the mother was picking up the HARD SELL message by her eager listening.

The salesman was quick to detect timing signals. This enabled him to maintain enthusiasm at a high pitch.

The salesman quickly and smoothly changed direction of his major sales presentation. This prevented business from slipping away. The switch brought the whole family into the selling process.

The key to that salesman's successful close was changing horses in midstream and keeping his presentation rolling toward his well-defined objective.

Secret of Clock Watching and How to Make It Pay

On the first job I ever had, I was warned about the evils of clock watching. "Watch the clock and lose your job," was the pet slogan of my philosophical boss. He was sincere about it. In one sense he was right. Clock watching can kill ambition. To become obsessed with joy in idleness is bound to discount the rewards of hard work. On the other hand, there is a way to make clock watching profitable.

Your clock registers the minutes and hours of the day. This, of course, is obvious, and those minutes and hours have only a fragile relationship to quitting time.

Your clock also registers production speed. That's different. For instance, through the simplicity of watching your clock you can count the minutes and the hours expended in landing a much-wanted sale.

Your clock registers the minute your early bird companion arrives on the job.

Your clock registers the hour, even the minute that you begin work.

Each job you perform has a time element in it. That boss of mine may have had this in mind when he warned me of the evils of clock watching. Had he been with me when I was striving to nail down a luscious account, he might have recognized a few of the virtues of clock watching. He might have come to the conclusion, as I did, that there actually is a SECRET OF CLOCK WATCHING MAGIC which pays off in selling. That element of magic power which pays off so well is neatly wrapped up in the MAGIC OF TIMING. That same element is related to the SECRET OF THE HARD SELL IN LANDING THE TOUGH ONES.

Now it is time for us to examine four significant tips about clock watching. These tips indicate how you can make the magic of clock watching pay off. NOTICE:

1. WATCH THE CLOCK and note the time that you discover to be the most favorable for confronting your hard-to-sell prospect.

2. WATCH THE CLOCK and note the time you should have spent today in HARD SELL effort but did not.

3. WATCH THE CLOCK and note the time you spent in the presence of a "cooperative" prospect and how well those minutes paid off.

4. WATCH THE CLOCK and make note of your most productive hours of the working day. Note how you made those hours pay off so well. Or, did they?

The magic power of such in-depth self-examination enables you to find the answers to two vital questions:

1. WHY did you succeed in closing that last sale and HOW did you do it?
2. WHY did your sales presentation fall flat at times and HOW could you have given it greater HARD SELL POWER?

The SECRET OF CLOCK WATCHING MAGIC lies within us. To sell more, we re-evaluate the dynamic power which nature has artfully concealed within the 24 hours allotted to each of us as a daily ration. The MAGIC OF TIMING lies in the skills we develop to increase our sales producing power. Through judicious use of eight or ten or 12 of the 24 hours allotted to each of us, we find the opportunities to master the *Secrets of the Hard Sell*. To grasp the significance of constructive clock watching, I suggest that we take time out to reread the four tips for making clock watching pay off for us. In those tips we note the following:

(Top billing has been given to hard-to-sell prospects. The reason: Those tough guys usually pay off well when they yield to our persuasive power.)

(We note that TIMING also has high billing. Jack Fowler kept a small book with notes in it about hard-to-sell prospects. He was eager to sell to those prospects. He made each call on them a matter of record. By clock watching, Fowler was able to note his good hours and his bad hours with those prospects. From his notebook record he was able to make a reasonable guess of the most favorable hour to tackle each of those prospects with a new idea. "This notebook has required only a few minutes of each day to keep it up," Fowler told me. "It saves valuable hours for me. From my notes I receive 'not now' signals. From those same notes of experience I receive the 'let's go' signals. Magic? Perhaps. At any rate, my sales record shows how profitable clock watching has been for me. It's my pet gimmick. It helps me keep up my sales volume. For me it has the magic power of kicking discouragement in the pants.")

George Culbert was in a business in which his average sales had been below $1,000. By clock watching and by recording the time spent with prospects and how well that time paid off, George told me, he had boosted his average sales total by making more calls more productively. He explained: "Cutting down on time required to close a sale became a worthwhile challenge to me. When I set up specific objectives and went after them, it worked. I condensed my presentations. I made them more meaningful to my prospects. I made them more colorful. This built interest in my product. I saved time for my prospects and for myself. As a result I sold more in less time."

You, too, can make the MAGIC OF CLOCK WATCHING pay off if you take the following steps:

1. Apply clock watching to improving your attitude toward your prospect and your product.
2. Use clock watching magic to capitalize on *Secrets of the Hard Sell.*
3. Use clock watching as a tool for deeper self-appraisal.
4. Use clock watching to realize how closely it is linked with the MAGIC OF TIMING.

When we combine the act of clock watching with the magic of timing we set up a power structure that thrives on difficult sales problems. This is a force, a magic power, which we detect behind the great successes in virtually every field of selling.

The dynamic force which surges within the minds of masters of the *Secrets of the Hard Sell* gets much of its productive energy from the MAGIC OF TIMING.

7

How to Mellow Stubborn Accounts with the Secret Power of Hard Sell Presentation

Some salesmen might call Dan Boller a "trouble shooter." That label doesn't do justice to Dan. He's a HARD SELL specialty salesman. He has hiked his income to the five-figure level. He has a record of persuading hard-to-sell prospects to buy. He takes on accounts that a lot of us shy away from. He has found the secret of mellowing contrary rascals who tax our patience.

We, who make our bread by selling, frequently encounter prospects of the bulldog type. When this happens, do we throw in the towel? Too many of us do. Too many of us prefer to tackle easier prey. Dan Boller operates differently. He goes for stubborn, argumentative, growling prospects. They tempt him. They challenge him. He gets all steamed up with this type of sales resistance. He goes after them with persistent, persuasive, HARD SELL enthusiasm. Moreover, Dan SELLS to those prospects whom others have rated as "too ornery to be sold."

Let's see how Dan goes about this:

He begins by facing realities.

He acknowledges that many hard-to-sell accounts are down-right obstinate.

Yet, Dan believes they are worth the fight. They are difficult to manage. They may discourage some of us. They challenge Dan.

Dan believes that he should match stubborn resistance with HARD SELL stubbornness. Recognizing that there is some virtue in stubbornness, Dan concludes that in order to sell to a stubborn prospect he will have to overwhelm that prospect. He will have to make it difficult for that prospect to resist buying. Therefore, he sets out to smother that prospect's anti-buying stubbornness with the SECRET POWER in HARD SELL PERSUASION.

Perhaps we should develop admiration for stubborn sales resistance. Dan shows such admiration. He says: "When I get the first hot blast from a hardened, tough prospect I attempt to mellow him. I know that a belligerent prospect seldom buys. My only hope is to warm him up. Make him friendly is my first objective.

"If I should wilt under the heat of a growling prospect's resistance to my proposal he'll get louder. He'll become harder to sell. He's enjoying throwing me off guard. But, he isn't making any money. At heart that fellow is just as eager to make money as I am. So why should I cheat him? Why shouldn't I give him the most friendly scrap he has ever experienced? For me, nothing makes the day more delightful than to close a sale I have fought for long and hard. Especially if that fight mellowed a tough prospect."

The SECRET of mellowing a stubborn account is this: (a) Show him how your product will make money for him. (b) Show him how your product will provide him with better living, more fun in life, greater prestige, or more efficiency in his business. The prospect of benefits usually thaws out ice barriers that hold up or kill sales. When your prospect shows his teeth, you need not feel helpless. You have an arsenal of selling tools in reserve. Here are some of those tools:

(a) You have SALES "GUTS." This fighting spirit can stir up a persuasive wave that is hot with mellowing HARD SELL POWER.

(b) You have HARD SELL WORDS. These words have magic power. With them you can give life to your presentations. You can provide drama for your demonstration. These words can provide dynamic power for your HARD SELL persuasive effort.

(c) You have TIME. There is magic selling power in timing. You can combat buying resistance by releasing soothing words at the right moment. You can TIME the dynamic points in your presentation for maximum effect.

(d) You can QUESTION your prospect. The thoughtful question often mellows a hostile prospect. With that in mind the HARD SELL QUIZ can provide you with magic selling power.

Several masters of the HARD SELL have explained to us that the greatest challenge to the HARD SELL principle pops up at the moment a sour prospect growls "NO!" Success in this maneuver depends on how well we handle the "NO" obstacle. First we must determine why he acts as he does. We must search out the answers to the following questions:

(a) What does our prospect really want? What's he after?

(b) Is he crying out for encouragement to buy?

(c) Is he fishing for some way to either reinforce or justify his stubborn resistance?

(d) Is he hungry for more information? Does what we have for sale intrigue him? Is he unwilling to admit his interest? Is he afraid that he might put himself on the spot if he gets too inquisitive?

(e) Could it be possible that our prospect actually wants us to encourage him to make up his mind? To say "YES"?

To handle our stubborn prospect we obviously must "get with him" in HARD SELL persuasion. We cannot resist him. This may antagonize him. The more certain, the more profitable approach probably will be to "sweeten" him with tempting, beneficial possibilities. In this situation, we put our diplomatic ability on the line. We can't win by snarling at our prospect, calling him "cockeyed" or demanding: "Now you listen to me!" This stubborn prospect isn't going to buy that. He isn't going to admit that he is cockeyed. He isn't going to pay attention just because you yell at him and demand that he listen. Nevertheless, some of us do flare back in that fashion. We try to beat down sales resistance with our own brand of stubbornness. The better way is this:

(a) Patiently dig in to expose the real reason for our prospect's resistance. This is a top level challenge to our persuasive ability.

(b) Make our stubborn prospect feel important. Never depreciate him. Tell him that his objection has merit. Show him that it has a selling point. Then convert that objection into a sale. That's the HARD SELL magic you'll put to work.

(c) Restate the most dynamic sales points we have presented. Be direct. Be specific. Show clearly how these points can benefit our prospect.

(d) Avoid argument. Be brief. Be persuasive. Be calm, pleasant. Smile through the whole ordeal, even when resistance is strongest. Let's keep our target in mind: To convince our stubborn prospect so thoroughly that we have what he needs that he'll enthusiastically buy.

The Principle: Squeeze every objection until it yields something to add to our own selling power. Welcome objections. Get them out in the open so we can evaluate them. In the final showdown, leave our prospect with the impression that his decision to buy was really his own idea. Never let him feel that he has been unduly pressured into buying.

Ingredients of the Secret Hot Line to Pull Down Sales Resistance

The thrill that never loses its excitement: Having a stubborn prospect yield to your selling power. It is one of the great rewards of salesmanship. I have experienced that thrill. One of my prospects became mellow and receptive. He did a complete about-face. His attitude changed toward me and my product.

Why did his attitude change? What ingredients had I put into my sales presentation that pulled down the obstacle that stood between me and my prospect?

It became evident to me that what we call "selling power" is a potent mixture of HARD SELL ingredients.

I have discussed this point with other salesmen. They had experienced similar sales situations and had overcome similar obstacles. Each of us asked: "Why did our prospects resist us in the first place?" We also asked: "Why did they mellow?" And, "What caused this change?" We continued to probe: "Why did our prospects eventually come around to our way of thinking? Why did they finally buy? What were the ingredients of our individual SECRET HOT LINES?"

The answer became relatively simple: (a) Our "hot line" ingredients had penetrating power. (b) Our "hot line" ingredients bored through the walls of sales resistance.

We evaluated those ingredients. We settled on five. We agreed that five ingredients had made up the potent mixture which had mellowed our stubborn accounts. Here are those five ingredients:

1. ATTENTION.
2. INTEREST.
3. NEED.
4. DESIRE.
5. DECISION.

Each of those five ingredients has magnetic power. That power draws our prospects nearer to us. For maximum impact we combine and use these ingredients in our sales presentations. Those ingredients, when skillfully employed, stimulate the impulse to buy. They weaken sales resistance.

ATTENTION is the number one ingredient. This may seem obvious to you. IT IS! Attention is a "must" if you propose to sell. It is the first secret of sales presentation. Get attention! SAY something. SHOW something. Or DO something that will attract favorable attention.

Success in selling may also come by accident, but you can't bet on it. An accident literally contributed to the success of an insurance counselor I knew. He was up against a stubborn prospect. Repeatedly he had been turned down by that prospect. Again and again he had returned in an effort to land that desirable account. Then an accident happened. That stubborn prospect's business associate was killed in an automobile accident. His family was penalized because he had neglected to protect them adequately with insurance. The example was painful. It registered with that stubborn prospect. This made it easier for the insurance salesman to get that prospect's attention. However, it did not eliminate the need for the HARD SELL follow-through. Four additional steps had to be taken:

INTEREST had to be sustained. Interest had to be heightened. So the salesman concentrated on the prospect's NEED for insurance. By factual and emotional presentations DESIRE had to be aroused. When desire reached its peak, its own magic power would bring about a DECISION that would close the sale.

When we apply those same five ingredients to pulling down sales resistance we will also discover that those *Secrets of the Hard Sell* are alive with magic power. With sales barriers down, our persuasive power becomes more effective. We mellow stubborn accounts. Then we venture into new fields. There we defy obstacles and develop sales in volume. To advance profitably, let us now examine six time-tested requirements for capitalizing on our victory over sales resistance. Here are those six requirements:

1. MAKE IT ENTICING. Tempt your prospect. Glorify your product or service. Dramatize projected benefits. Be positive. Be persuasive. Be enthusiastic. Convince your prospect so well that he really believes that "this is the way."

2. MAKE IT CLEAR. Remove any foggy notions about the value of what you have to sell. Anticipate objections. Answer them before your prospect throws them at you.

3. MAKE IT COMPLETE. Tell all. Leave nothing for after-thought doubts to feed on. Present every detail

of what you have to sell with interest-compelling clarity.

4. MAKE IT CONVINCING. Whatever you say, make it ring with truth. Nail down every claim you make for your product. Support every claim you make. Prove those claims. Present facts and examples to clinch your case.

5. MAKE IT DRAMATIC. Give your imagination an open field. Turn it loose. Put color into your presentation. Be spectacular. Be different. Innovate. Don't be timid. Showmanship has magic selling power. This is the essence of BOLD SELLING.

6. WIDEN YOUR PROSPECT'S FIELD. Give him a choice. Capitalize on the "this or that" principle. Ask him: "Which do you prefer, this or that?" This enlarges his field. It broadens his vision. You offer him a choice of two or three. Seldom more than three. Too many choices confuse. Your prospect is now about to make a choice of buying or not buying. If he chooses one the decision is his. The outcome rests with your skill in HARD SELL CLOSING.

The Principle:—Use "rifle-shot" selling in every case. "Rifle-shot" selling fires straight at the bull's eye. You have chosen your target—your prospective buyer. The bull's eye you are aiming at is a closed sale. Effective "rifle-shot" selling is another of the *Secrets of the Hard Sell.* Here's how we make this effective: We fire away with (a) persuasive, convincing speech; (b) with visual aids that clarify and entice; (c) with examples (proof) of how others have reaped benefits by investing in what we have for sale.

Attention-Arresters That Open Doors to Admit Secret Hard Sell Power

I was seated in the waiting room of a large clinic when I saw how getting attention also gets you in to see your prospect. While I was there, an immaculately-dressed salesman came in. He presented his card to the receptionist. Eyes of the sick, the near-sick and others were on this man. He was distinctive. He stood out. He made a favorable impression. He told the receptionist that he had something new that the doctor would be anxious to see. He glanced at his watch, indicating time was valuable to him. The receptionist stepped into an office and when she returned the salesman was ushered into the presence of his prospect. That salesman would have been out of line had he used any type of noise making device to gain attention in a clinic. However, in some situations, the "gimmicks of the trade" are effective. In those cases they open hard-to-open doors. At the same time, it is good HARD SELL procedure to be discriminating in any bid for attention.

I recall a salesman who sold chain saws. He came into a dealer's place of business shuffling a pack of playing cards. This got attention. The dealer snickered: "We hire no card dealers in this place." The salesman smiled. "I know," he replied, "but you do sell chain saws to a lot of poker-playing lumberjacks." Thus the sales door had been opened on good terms. The salesman showed what his house was doing to stimulate sales for chain saw dealers. He pointed out that the back of each of those playing cards carried a special message to chain saw users. The salesman had the dealer interested. He went on to show how the playing cards he was shuffling had a direct effect on the dealer's pocketbook. As a result, he closed a substantial sale. He sweetened the sale with an allotment of "free" playing cards which that dealer could take with him into the timber country where his prospects were.

Showmanship generally is a great attention-arrester. Even the pharmaceutical salesman was an effective showman. He carried himself with impressive dignity. His mannerisms got attention. He was not intrusive. With the receptionist he was firm, yet quietly persistent. An anxious glance at his watch indicated that time was important. The receptionist acted to get him in to see the doctor. She got the message. Showmanship? Indeed, it was. Refined showmanship.

A wholesale candy salesman captures attention by tempting his prospects with an open box of his product. "Taste these new bonbons we are introducing," he says. He follows this up with intriguing prospects of profit for the dealer. "This is a new development in our candy-making," he explains. "The candy is new. The packaging is new. The flavors are new. This is super-delicious candy, as you can now testify. Have another one." He passes the open box to the dealer and to the young lady behind the confectionery counter. "Look at these sales records," he continues. "All the way across my territory this candy is turning out to be a best seller."

Taste, color, uniqueness or any action that fixes interest on your product can become an attention-arrester. It can open doors to permit you to release your full HARD SELL POWER.

For maximum selling power, we make our products or services the focal point of our presentations. A display advertising salesman from the newspaper grabs his prospect's attention with a simple, yet effective approach: "This is how your name will show up in this advertisement. I prepared this layout so you could visualize how thousands of readers will see your ad. They will buy your merchandise because this ad has strong selling power. Don't you agree?"

Likewise, the billboard salesman presents an appealing sketch with selling impact to grab the attention of his prospect.

A TV salesman takes his prospect to a presentation studio. There he shows him how he will appear in action in his own commercial. This gets satisfying attention of many prospects. It also sells TV time.

A radio salesman lets his prospect hear a reproduction of his own voice. "This is how your voice will sound to thousands of our listeners. You have a strong voice. It's very appealing. I wanted you to hear it." Believe me, this sells spot commercial time.

Let's check the following SECRETS of getting the sort of attention that will invite your HARD SELL POWER to get in its profit-making licks:

1. Show your product in use. Dwell on convenience. Dramatize ease of operation. Show why it saves time.

2. Employ showmanship. Make it easy and interesting for your prospect to visualize how he can benefit by buying what you have to sell.

3. Glorify unique features of your product. Glorify color. Glorify flavor. Glorify design. Glorify sturdi-

ness. Glorify any feature that can promise benefits
to your prospect.

4. Let your prospect taste, smell, feel, see, or hear your
   product. The striking of a clock, for instance, has
   HARD SELL power when you cause it to strike at
   the right minute, under the right circumstances.

5. Dress for the occasion. To attract the favorable at-
   tion of a banker, be neat. Wear tailored clothes. Be
   clean shaven. Put on your jeans to go into the forest
   to sell your product to lumberjacks.

Principle:—Attention-arresters are included among the *Secrets of the Hard Sell*. Those with self-interest appeal head the
list. They are the ones with the magic power of the HARD SELL.
Exploit all features of your product which promise benefits to your
prospects.

How to Involve Your Prospect by Pitching
with the Magic Power of Hard Sell

When your prospect surrenders to your contagious enthusiasm
he takes the first step toward buying. He becomes involved in the
selling process. Some of the most stubbornly resisted sales are
closed by prospect involvement and by persuasive showmanship.

A retail salesman came to my attention when he received a
special award for his consistent record in selling household appli-
ances. I had seen that salesman in action. On one occasion, a
woman came to him to examine a new model refrigerator. At once
he persuaded her to monkey with the many new gadgets. He pulled
out shelves for her. He opened whole storage sections. "See how
easy it is to clean this refrigerator," he said to the woman. "Notice,
you have quick and easy access to any food you want to reach.
This refrigerator has more exclusive features than any refrigerator
now on the market regardless of price." By this time, that salesman
had the woman prying into every corner of that refrigerator. He had
her deeply involved. She was having a good time. She became so
involved that when the salesman asked her what day and at what

hour delivery of the refrigerator would be the most convenient for her she gleefully cooperated.

On another occasion I saw the magic power of the HARD SELL work for a typewriter salesman. He had been calling on an office manager who had stubbornly resisted getting involved with the newest model machine. The salesman tried another approach. He placed one of his new models on the desk of the executive secretary. He asked her to try it. He called her attention to the newest features. He left the machine with her for a day. He wanted her to get the "feel" of it. She had complete freedom to "do her thing" with that machine. She became totally involved. She also became eager and enthusiastic. She went with the salesman to the office manager. Excitedly she told the office manager how production could be improved if they had this new typewriter. She was now speaking his language. Better production hit his self-interest nerve. She did this better than the salesman could have done it. The upshot was that the sales manager became convinced. He was sold so thoroughly that he bought a whole battery of the typewriters. All this resulted because that salesman got a competent secretary involved in the sale of his product.

Automobile salesmen who fail to get their prospects involved lose HARD SELL power. The HARD SELL salesman first gets his prospect behind the wheel. Until a prospect gets the thrill of driving a new car, he (or she) is still toying with excuses for not buying now. One salesman with a record of consistent high sales once remarked: "I sell more cars behind the steering wheel than under the engine hood." He said that the "feel" was the thing that sold cars. Behind the wheel, the prospect gets a feeling of power. He gets a status feeling. He becomes somebody. He gets a feeling of pride. He goes on to try out the gadgets on the instrument panel. He tries out the braking power on his first test ride. He feels the security of power steering. He understands the safety features. He has been told how they fit into the construction of that car. And, he believes it. He becomes convinced that the car has been designed for his personal comfort. For his pleasure. For his safety. All this has happened because that salesman got that prospect involved. He bought that car because that salesman exposed him to the magic power in *Secrets of the Hard Sell*.

The Principle:—Tie in your product with the best interests of your prospect. When we show our prospects how they can benefit, we have gone halfway toward closing a sale. When we persuade them to prove our claims by trying our product, we break down stubborn sales resistance. Prospect involvement is the sure-fire step to do this. Prospect involvement is HARD SELL magic. Prospect involvement permits a prospect to literally "sell" himself.

How Mellowed Tough Ones Sell Themselves When Hard Sell Persuasion Draws Them In

One SECRET of closing sales with prospects who were once tough, but are now mellowed, is by REVERSE SELLING. This method of taking command of a difficult selling situation has raised salesmen into "stardom." One real estate salesman added $10,000 to his annual income by reverse selling. A specialty salesman mastered reverse selling and closed big-ticket sales which he once believed were impossible. An investment broker trained his staff in reverse selling when he found out that it has MAGIC HARD SELL POWER.

What, then, is this SECRET OF THE HARD SELL?

1. It is the art of generating self-selling power within your prospect.
2. It is high level prospect involvement.
3. It is high level persuasion without appearing to be obtrusive.

We can generate self-selling power within our prospects by a combination of high-level persuasion and high-level prospect involvement. As one successful salesman in the advertising field explained: "Reverse selling is the art of buck passing for profit. You plant the seeds. You hope they will sprout into a sale. You let your prospect take over. If you have fed him well on enthusiasm he'll work himself up to a sale. If you have fed him well on self-interest possibilities in your proposal, he'll buy. Persuade him to talk. Allow him full sway in discussion. Make this his show. Avoid argument. Don't intrude. Listen until there is evidence of total decision. Then close."

Three do's and only one don't in drawing prospects into the selling process:

> DO THIS: Persuade your prospect to talk. Allow your prospect full opportunity for discussion. Make this his show.
>
> WATCH YOUR STEP: Don't argue. Don't intrude when your prospect is expounding.
>
> DO .THIS: Listen! Let him talk himself into buying. Watch carefully for evidence that he thinks he has come to a decision.
>
> DO THIS: Move in for the close! Keep the dialogue going until he initials the order.

Reverse selling is a product of HARD SELL PERSUASION. Let us assume that our prospect has been sold on the merits of our proposal. But, being of stubborn mind, he doesn't readily submit to our persuasion. He continues to nurse some of his pet objections. This happened with a tire salesman I knew. He had been bidding for a large fleet-order. The fleet operator had been stubbornly resisting buying. The salesman had succeeded in getting partial agreement on some of the most vital points relating to his tires. At this point he launched into what we call "reverse selling." He said to the fleet operator: "I suggest that you take this data I have prepared for you. Go over it carefully. See if it doesn't suggest a way for you to come out ahead on your tire cost per mile." That suggestion pecked at the fleet operator's pocketbook. He became involved. With pencil in hand he became more involved. He jotted down figures. He asked questions. The salesman gave him solid, factual replies. He provided more evidence to support his proposal. Finally the fleet operator leaned back in his chair and said: "I've touched every base. I can't beat your deal. How soon can you get a large bulk shipment to me?"

The HARD SELL is a persuasive magnet. It differs from the fist-pounding, foot-stomping, pitched-voice sales pitch. The HARD SELL is a soothing, confidence-winning, captivating presentation that draws your prospect to the buying point. Your persuasive presentation is loaded with impressive, undeniable facts. It is alive with ideas having alluring, profit-making possibilities for your prospect. Or, it may be alive with tempting ideas for a better way of life for your prospect.

It is the HARD SELL that mellows the hard-to-sell prospect. When ideas are dramatically presented and products are vividly demonstrated, our prospects "see" what we want them to see. In this there is HARD SELL persuasion. There is BOLD SHOWMANSHIP. The combination gets attention. We make it all appear to be so desirable. It makes resistance more difficult for our prospect. It makes buying the natural thing to do. This is our objective. This is the result if we fit it all into the needs and plans of our prospect. Then he wants it, badly. And, another SECRET OF THE HARD SELL has done its job!

After The Sale Is Made What New Secrets Are in Store for You?

One of my friends was a veteran salesman of printing equipment. He knew his line well. I knew he had closed a sale in my town only a few months before. Now he was back again. He said: "That fellow is doing a great job with that new press I installed for him. It's making money for him, too. I can see how he can make more money, so I want to remain very close to him. That explains why I'm back in town so soon. I see possibilities of one or two more pieces of equipment going into his shop in the immediate future. Right now, I'm taking the long-range approach. I'm working on him to go after more printing business. He hasn't developed business here as he should. If I can sell him on that idea, I'll soon be selling him more equipment. He needs to push his sales people to become more creative. I'm afraid they're just taking orders, not really selling."

One sale often leads to another. This is even true among "order-takers." They drop in on accounts about the time supplies previously bought are exhausted. The salesman writes another order and says "goodbye" until the next trip. This is contrary to the HARD SELL idea. *Secrets of the Hard Sell* include repeated call-backs. Through creative selling our prospects become first-time customers. By imaginative HARD SELL follow-ups those customers grow into more substantial accounts. By serving those accounts with constructive ideas they prosper and so do we. We will never appreciate how new SECRETS come to light and make money for us unless we keep our HARD SELL lines of communication open and active.

As a planning guide for finding out what SECRETS may be in store for you after a sale is closed consider the following five keys to HARD SELL SUCCESS:

1. REPETITION.—This is the secret of pyramiding sales with old and new accounts. Tell them often. Sell them over and over again.

2. IDEAS.—Enrich these with profit-making possibilities. This is the self-interest secret of developing sales in volume. Become known as a dependable "idea man."

3. GOAL-SETTING.—Make it imaginative. This is the secret of finding out *how* we stand in relation to our own operations. Aim high! Set goals that dare you to achieve greatness.

4. RESOURCEFULNESS.—This is the secret of introducing exploration into selling. Explore all avenues to convert sales obstacles into sales. Find that better way to sell more.

5. ENTHUSIASM.—This is the secret of introducing excitement into selling. You'll sell more when your enthusiasm is at fever heat. The fever is contagious, too.

8

Stage Secrets That Put Selling Punch into Your Demonstrations

A salesman and a trial lawyer have something in common. Both of them conduct demonstrations to prove a point. Perhaps this explains why: Demonstration is the "highest form of proof" according to one eminent authority. Accepting that as a fact, then, we sell ourselves short if we fail to demonstrate how our products can benefit our prospects.

"Let me show you" should be our direct bid for consideration or reconsideration of our proposals. Few prospects refuse to "take a look." It's buying they resist. "Let me show you" is HARD SELL SHOWMANSHIP. It leads to buying.

I heard an aggressive trial lawyer invite a jury to "take a look." He did this to assure himself that the jury was with him in his argument. "Let me show you," he said. Then he demonstrated how the point he had made was pertinent. In this "look-see" step, he was "selling" the jury on a pertinent point that he considered to be favorable to his client. In driving that point home, he was actually employing a SECRET OF THE HARD SELL.

Showmanship adds selling punch to your demonstrations. It makes them stage performances. By a bit of acting you grab attention. You stimulate interest in your product. You show and prove how your product can benefit your prospect. Showmanship has strengthened your prospect's conviction of the merits of your product. By showmanship you arouse desire for your product. You show your prospect why he has a need for what you have to sell. You convince him and he buys. Showmanship has put HARD SELL MAGIC into your demonstration.

You may be a rose fancier. You have roses for sale. You say those roses are beautiful. Perhaps your prospect disagrees with you. Perhaps you will have to prove your point if you intend to sell those roses. Perhaps you should glorify those roses.

You may be a coffee salesman. You may say that your brand of coffee is good. Showmanship can make it superior to a majority of your prospects. Take the case of "Mrs. Olsen." She is a TV personality. She is a coffee-brewing housewife. She does more than sell coffee. She demonstrates that only one brand of coffee can do the job. She smiles as she works in the kitchen. She sniffs the steaming coffee. She shows great delight over the aroma of her favorite coffee. She tells you, her prospect, that "you can almost taste the aroma." She involves coffee-drinkers and potential coffee-drinkers in her act. She further glorifies her product by the no-effort appeal: "It's so easy to make good coffee," she says. She goes on to show you how this is done with her brand of coffee. She became convincing by showing you that it really is "so easy." Her coffee "smelled so good you could almost taste the aroma." And up go her coffee sales!

Showmanship also has "heart appeal." This requires more than telling. It calls for showing. This impact is the product of creative, imaginative presentation of what you have for sale. The most successful salesmen profit by developing the art of dramatic presentation. They put color and life into their presentations. They use demonstration as a HARD SELL tool because it persuades prospects to buy.

There are SECRETS of producing HARD SELL demonstrations. We can master those secrets. SHOWMANSHIP is one of those SECRETS. Showmanship may come quite naturally. "Mrs. Olsen" acted quite natural when she showed us how to make good coffee. You, too, can put your product in the center of the stage. You, too, can bring your product, and yourself, and your prospect, into the act. Then you have the makings of a HARD SELL "act." As a further guide to making your next sales demonstration pay off check the following SECRETS of producing HARD SELL demonstrations:

1. EXCITEMENT.—Get excitement into your act. This is the opposite of apathy. It squelches dullness. It arouses interest. It creates wants. It suggests needs. It is the "come alive" SECRET OF THE HARD SELL.

2. VIVIDNESS.—Make it brilliant. Give it action. Put life into it. Make your demonstrations strong and distinctive. Make it so vivid that your selling point shines brighter than any doubt that might arise.

3. IMPRESSIVENESS.—Turn the lights on your product. Glorify it. Make it appear to be important to your prospect. Impress him with its value. Impress him with its possible benefits to him (or to her).

4. MOVEMENT.—Put sparkle into your demonstration. Relate several instances of beneficial use. Draw people into the drama you are creating. Involve them. This gives your demonstration life. It gives your demonstration movement. It makes it a HARD SELL show.

5. EMOTION.—A touch of sentiment can lift your demonstration out of the "so, so" class. It can give it "star" quality. Emotional appeal has magic power in selling. A tug at the heart strings often yields high dividends in the market place.

6. CONFLICT.—In conflict lies the secret of drama. This SECRET captures and holds interest. You can pit the hard way of life against the easier way. You can sell many products on that dramatic pitch alone. Conflict is a natural for the HARD SELL demonstration. Note these, for instance: Cheapness vs. quality. . . . Gayety vs. dullness. . . . Commonplace vs. exclusiveness. . . . The hard life vs. leisurely luxury. . . . Profits tomorrow vs. the fast buck today. . . . A survival job vs. a career. . . . Color vs. black and white. . . . You can drive it in two days vs. you can fly there in two hours.

The Art of Steering Demonstrations Toward the Buying Point with Hard Sell Demonstrations

The most effective sales demonstrations are more than "teasers." By relating your product or service to your prospect you give your demonstration magic power. You give it momentum. To achieve this effect, you make your demonstration intriguing.

When you are admitted to the presence of a first-time prospect, your first objective is to grab his attention. Favorably, that is. Already his trip-hammer mind is at work. He's thinking more about you than about what you have to sell. He's asking himself: "How do I ease this guy out of here?" However, if you have succeeded in grabbing his attention at the outset, you have gained a foothold. Hang on to it. Your next move: Intensify his interest. *Next:* Sustain that interest. *Next:* Develop that first flicker of interest that you detected into warm buying interest. *Next:* Fan that buying interest into a buying flame. *Next:* Close with the HARD SELL POWER you have reserved within you for this dramatic moment. It's the pay-off moment for you.

In any dramatic presentation, we literally take our prospects on a trip to the buying point. To accomplish this we have had our target clearly in mind. We have steered our demonstration toward a pre-chosen target. This is the technique we have called "rifle-shot" selling.

Hard sell dramatization aims to show prospects *how* or *why* they can benefit by buying what we have to sell. Dramatic showmanship can make our product appealing. Constructive showmanship can enlighten our prospects. Such enlightenment can feed our prospects with the desire to possess what we have to sell.

Generally, people are more responsive to being shown than to being told. Prospects respond to imaginative showmanship. Trying to tell them what they should do often stiffens sales resistance. Showmanship can soften such resistance. We find that many prospects are somewhat like children. They become amazed at little things that appeal to their fancy. They become interested in new things. If we permit them to touch our product they become more interested in it. If we can show our product in use our prospects become still more interested. If our product can be manipulated by our prospects their interest increases.

We need not become clowns to produce effective dramatic demonstrations. We need not try to imitate Red Skelton, although he demonstrated how effective showmanship can be. We need only to be sincere, natural, and to activate our product. Show how it works. Show how our prospects can use it. Show what it has done for others. To do this most effectively, we try to involve our prospects in the demonstration. This often shifts the demonstration into high gear. When this happens, we are headed toward our pre-chosen sales target—to close the sale.

For a moment, let us turn back to yesterday. Let us see what we can learn that will yield dividends for us in today's selling. I once saw a street vendor selling hair restorer. He went into action under a light in a village street. There he set up his display. This attracted a crowd. People were asking: "What's going on here?" Already that salesman had created mass interest. He then set up large pictures of men staring at strands of hair caught in the teeth of a comb. These were pictures of "the disaster of falling hair." This was the theme of his sales pitch. These pictures provided the backdrop for that salesman's display of his product. This display was made up of open cases of large bottles of his hair restorer.

Time came for the salesman to do his thing. He sounded a gong. The crowd moved in closer. He pointed to the pictures and shouted: "This man here once had no more hair on his head than you'd find on a fortune-teller's crystal ball. Then he used this magic hair restorer and this was the result." The salesman poured his "restorer" on his own hair-covered head. "Look what this has done for me," he shouted. "I was once a real skinhead."

Then this showman-salesman made a pitch to the women in the crowd. "There are mighty few wives of bald-headed men who haven't at some time wished their husband's hair would come back again." This involved many of the women. Now he offered his "magic tonic" to that amazed crowd. They bought. Some took two and three bottles. In an hour, his stock had been sold. But he assured the people he had another shipment coming in. He'd be back the next night. He was and the crowd was even larger. But that was his closing night.

Whether we admire that curbstone salesman's method or not, he did have some virtues that can become profitable to us. Here are some HARD SELL points he used. They created sales. We, too, can profit by them:

(a) He dramatized his sales presentation.

(b) He was always interesting. He sustained interest.

(c) He showed as he told his prospects *how* and *why*.

(d) He involved his prospects.

We need not be "hams" to profit by dramatic presentations. But, we do need to maintain interest in our product. We need to dramatize what it will do for our prospects. We need never to be boring. We need to hold a firm grip on our prospects' interests as the old-timer did. He steered his demonstration steadily toward the buying point with HARD SELL dramatization.

Tomorrow morning when you start out to beat today's sales record you can do this and profit by it:

(a) Stir up your power of imagination. Stimulate it.

(b) Come up with logical, attainable, profit-making ideas for your prospects.

(c) Do something to capture and hold the attention of your prospects.

(d) Carry something with you that will create interest in what you have to sell.

A sales representative for a radio station carried with him a small radio. He had this radio tuned in on the station he represented and it was playing. This became a "launching pad" for his presentations of why his prospects could profit by buying commercial spots on that station.

A sales representative for a calendar production house carried a huge roll under his arm. It was an over-size calendar. This jumbo-size roll evoked questions, such as: "What's that?" This threw the door open for that salesman to sell "indoor billboards" to his prospects. That salesman was a top runner in sales volume.

Principle:—Creative imagination is a highly marketable product, regardless of the line we carry. Dramatic presentations do produce sales. They are top-rated among *Secrets of the Hard Sell.*

How a Dramatic Idea Can Capture and Hold Your Prospect's Interest

A dynamic personality named Frank Wester had an idea that captured the attention of people who were ready to buy. Wester was a demolition expert. He switched and became a HARD SELL genius. The sprawling Farragut Naval Training Station had been closed. Its site on the shores of Lake Pond Oreille in Idaho was an inviting spot with sales possibilities in the eyes of Frank Wester. He took on the liquidation of that naval installation. He sold the cantonment buildings house by house. He moved homes intact to prepared sites in Washington's rich Palouse wheat country and to other points in Idaho and Washington. When he had sold the buildings, he built new ones on his display site near the training station. He hauled those buildings to buyers' land to pre-prepared foundations. Homes, motels, churches, retail shops, bowling lanes are among the monuments to Frank Wester's vision and selling power. He sold his idea to bankers to make financing possible for his prospective customers. He sold his idea to those who could profit by his product and they bought. He converted open acreage into a tempting display center. This attracted buyers from three states and western Canada. He demonstrated to those prospects what he could do for them. He put over his idea through the persuasive power in *Secrets of the Hard Sell*.

Coleman duPont once made this point, so pertinent to us who sell:

"There are certain fundamental principles which, once thoroughly mastered, can be utilized in almost any line of business."

To capture interest, to hold interest, to capitalize on interest is our HARD SELL objective. Here is the 4-point secret of attaining that objective:

1. A DRAMATIC IDEA.—Dress it up. Make it believable. Make it desirable.

2. GIVE YOUR IDEA LIFE.—Glorify it. Dramatize it. Activate it.

3. DEMONSTRATE IT.—Show how your idea works. Show how it fits into your prospect's life. Show how it has benefited others.

4. PROOF.—Explain how your idea can benefit your prospect. Show how your prospect can capitalize on your idea. Make it clear. Make it seem possible. Make it persuasive.

We capture and hold the interest of prospects by appealing to their self-interest. This motivates them to try to attain their own objectives. This is the persuasive power in self-interest. Most of us are dominated by self-interest. We may have difficulty identifying this potent force in selling, but it's there! Regardless of status, our prospects are largely motivated by self-interest. Convince a sick man that you can make him well and you have his interest. Tell a man that you have the SECRET of getting rich and he'll listen. Convince him and he'll buy.

How Showmanship Holds the Key to the Magic Power in the Hard Sell

A crippled shoe repair man demonstrated in his one-man business how effective showmanship can become. Business was good for him. He thought it could be better. So, he had an idea. He prepared a demonstration shoe. This was a cut-away model. It showed what could be done to restore a shoe, instead of just repairing it. His demonstration showed *how* a complete re-build job would restore near-newness to a shoe. He told his people that half-soles did only "half a job." The result: An uptrend in rebuild jobs for this cobbler. In the first month of HARD SELL demonstration, this crippled cobbler increased his gross business by 20 percent. Today, most progressive shoe rebuilders provide similar demonstrations for customers. The crippled cobbler demonstrated that showmanship holds the key to the magic power in the HARD SELL. What that crippled cobbler did in his small way we can do on a much larger scale. The guiding principle is the same whether we are selling shoe rebuilding or big ticket investments. In either case, we can do as the crippled cobbler did. We can sell benefits to the buyer. We can increase our sales by vivid demonstrations. These are among the tested *Secrets of the Hard Sell.*

Here is the 3-way high voltage hook-up that consistently yields sales growth in both tangibles and intangibles:

1. HARD SELL DEMONSTRATION.—This is the convincing "let me show you" angle that puts punch in your persuasive selling.

2. HARD SELL SHOWMANSHIP.—Here we have the life-blood of high-spirited, captivating demonstrations. We find that most of us have been bitten by the stage bug. Instinctively we act out our parts. When we let our hair down and we are enthusiastic

about our product, our prospects respond. We get results. This is HARD SELL showmanship. It is one of the SECRETS of high-producing salesmen with top incomes.

3. BOLD SELLING.—Showmanship and demonstration require bold selling to produce sales. Bold selling is the firm, positive, enthusiastic approach to a sales problem. Bold selling amounts to a "frontal attack" on sales barriers. It cracks excuses for not buying. Bold selling, supplemented by demonstration and showmanship, produces sales.

In virtually all *Secrets of the Hard Sell,* the persuasive touch of showmanship has a part. Persuasive showmanship is an outgoing force. We *show* how to use and how to benefit by using what we have to sell. The "how" angle is "come on" showmanship. It works on our prospects.

Then we have "daring" showmanship. This works on us. It is a foe of timidity. Few ailments are as fatal to salesmen as timidity and fear. "Daring" showmanship is "stir up" salesmanship. It arouses us to action. One good, successful act of "daring" showmanship becomes a "shot in the arm" for many salesmen. They become amazed at their own dramatic power and its possibilities. "Daring" showmanship subdues the ghosts which haunt salesmen. Among these sales-killing gremlins are fears of self-styled "tough" prospects. Even the toughest prospects yield to "daring" showmanship. When we turn ourselves loose in bold selling, we develop "can do it" fever. This takes over and our trembling bodies become steady with HARD SELL POWER.

A salesman for one of the giant van lines in the moving industry went after business with a "can do it" attitude. He approached the door of a prospect with confidence that he already had the contract for the job, although that detail was yet to be accomplished. With that confident attitude he rang the door bell. When the prospect responded, the salesman was in the act of measuring the doorway. This grabbed the interest of the prospect. "What do you think you're up to?" she asked. "I'm the van line representative," he replied. "I was measuring your door to see what problems you have for us. If I may just step inside and measure your largest furniture pieces, please." This was daring salesmanship—a can-do follow up on a telephone inquiry. It was positive showmanship. That salesman brushed aside all doubt and fear of losing that account. He took the positive approach. Finally, he got around to talking about the cost of moving. When he had covered all the relative details of the undertaking he wrapped up the sale.

That van line salesman by showmanship and the magic power in the HARD SELL caused his sales volume to climb up and up. He lectured on his technique of BOLD SELLING to other salesmen in the organization. His tape-in-hand technique was attention-arresting. At that point he took over with a dramatic, yet simple, demonstration of how his "specialists" would ease those choice pieces of furniture through that almost too-narrow doorway and into the van "without a mar" of any kind. He showed no doubt about who was going to do the hauling. He simply assumed that his firm was. And, bold selling caused the housewife to nod in agreement.

The van line salesman was putting one of the *Secrets of the Hard Sell* to work for him. The soundness of this secret finds support in what a Chinese philosopher once said: "He is strong who conquers others; he who conquers himself is mighty."

How to Detonate Your Hard Sell Bomb with a Barrage of Hard Sell Facts

Woodrow Wilson once declared "there are whole worlds of facts awaiting to be discovered by inference." This is important to us who sell. We deal in facts. Or, we should. We can detonate our HARD SELL "bombs" if we lay down a barrage of facts containing dramatic sales appeal.

When I sold my home, I listed the property with a "hard fact" real estate agent. He brought a parade of prospects to see my home. He gave them hard facts about the place. Then a young man came to me one day. He was looking for a home. I referred him to my real estate agent. He returned with his own agent, who had cleared the matter with my agent. The prospect's agent confined his presentation largely to two facts—a large living room and a workshop adjacent to the garage. Instead of enumerating fact after fact, this agent laid down a barrage of dramatic facts. Result: He sold my place that night to the prospect. He did this by the HARD SELL. He did this by dramatizing the selling points that meant the most to that prospect.

We can detonate our HARD SELL "bombs" with a barrage of dramatic facts. We can be selective in using facts. The following HARD SELL FACTS point the way to capitalizing on dramatic facts:

1. Concentrate on *one big fact*. Make this fact vital to your prospect. Dramatize it.

2. Support your big fact with other related facts. Make these "extra" facts a bonus, supporting and magnifying the glory of the big fact.

3. Show (demonstrate) how these facts affect your prospect. Show him how he can benefit from these facts. Build those facts up. Make those facts so important that they cannot be passed over lightly.

4. Dramatize the uses of every fact. Make each fact vital to your prospect. Relate each fact to the big fact.

5. Tell and show how your prospect can benefit by every fact you present. Support your estimates and calculations with HARD SELL facts. Draw near to your prospect's pocketbook by dramatizing money facts. Dramatize possibilities of monetary benefits. Simplify money problems. Give your facts the magic of HARD SELL power all the way.

How can we dramatize a lifeless object? For instance, how can we dramatize a house? What's the secret of dramatizing cold facts? The answer is simple. The secret of dramatizing anything is ENTHUSIASM. The big secret among *Secrets of the Hard Sell* is ENTHUSIASM.

Walter P. Chrysler once declared: "The real secret of success is enthusiasm."

Sterling W. Sill, who demonstrates the magic power of enthusiasm in a soft, convincing, persuasive manner, assures us that "ENTHUSIASM wakes us up and makes us vital and untiring."

We can detonate our HARD SELL "bomb" with a barrage of dramatic facts. We can do this better with enthusiasm. To do this we must believe we can. We need to get "worked up" about what we are selling. It's invigorating to get "carried away" by our own ideas. It's a great feeling to explode with enthusiasm. It's a great feeling to see a prospect get hooked by the same enthusiasm. It's a memorable moment when your prospect gets "carried away" by your enthusiastic presentation. It's a thrill when he grabs your pen and signs a commitment to buy.

These things do happen. They happen when high voltage enthusiasm takes over in a sales situation.

9

Turning a Price Squeeze into a Bonanza with the Secret Power of the Hard Sell

Have you ever been caught in a price squeeze? It's a most realistic experience in selling. It can become a stimulating challenge for you. Moreover it can pay off in a big way for you!

One of my hard-selling friends was caught in a price squeeze. It became a bonanza for him. He picked up the challenge with the gallantry of a true master of the HARD SELL. He capitalized on the price squeeze, turning it into profit for himself. This is how he accomplished it:

(a) When his prospect made price the big issue, that salesman bore down on him by glorifying the features of his product. He showed how the prospect might be denying himself the benefits promised by those special features. This struck at the prospect's most vulnerable spot—his self-interest.

(b) The salesman ignored price. He worked around it. He built up interest in quality. He demonstrated the durability of his product. He played on the prospect's pride. He made capital out of "what will the people think?" He soon discovered that the prospect was quite human. He enjoyed being admired by others. He was anxious to make a more favorable impression. This desire soon overshadowed price consideration.

131

The price-squeeze problem became less treacherous to that salesman as he fought to subdue it by the HARD SELL. He discovered that too many salesmen fear the price squeeze. "A price squeeze can scare you," he admitted. "But you can grit your teeth and scare the ghost away and go right on selling."

In many instances, the price squeeze is used as a weapon by prospects. They use price wrangling to put salesmen on the spot. What the price-squeeze is implying is this: "Cut your price or else." Such an ultimatum should not, and does not, impress the master of the HARD SELL.

Two important issues are involved in the ordinary price squeeze. First is PRICE. That's the prospect's talking point. Then we have VALUE. That's where you come in with bonanza possibilities. You show the price-conscious prospect how he can actually cheat himself by putting his money into CHEAPNESS. You demonstrate to him the value and the pleasure he can enjoy by INVESTING in what might be called DEARNESS.

We may confuse some individual price-squeeze efforts with the big ticket price squeeze. The latter is frequently encountered in bidding for large chunks of business. In a bidding situation, quality and value are usually specified in the requirements. In those situations, specified quality becomes part of the price picture. An individual prospect, using a price squeeze, invariably has his eye only on the price tag. Everything else is incidental. This viewpoint yields readily to the magic power in the HARD SELL.

In a bulk-bidding situation, the field salesman may be left out of the deal. Negotiations may be carried on at executive levels. Nevertheless, field salesmen get caught in formidable price squeezes. These become as challenging and as competitive as bulk bidding.

The real estate salesman is a wide open target for a price squeeze. He operates in a highly competitive market. He sells in a competitive way. Price squeezes are not new to him. He capitalizes on them by mastering the *Secrets of the Hard Sell*.

The automobile salesman is under constant price pressure. In many instances he invites it. The "better deal" seems to be the pitch of the day in the automobile market.

Almost everything that is sold today is to some extent subject to a price squeeze. As a salesman, your problem boils down to this: *How can you break a price squeeze and capitalize on it?*

Solving your problem need not be too complicated. That problem has been solved and will continue to be solved by aggressive, imaginative, courageous salesmen using the MAGIC POWER IN THE HARD SELL. Salesmen often turn the price squeeze into a bonanza for themselves by tackling the problem head on. To clarify the problem further, consider these four elements:

1. PRICE.—In a price squeeze, the buyer's notion about price and the seller's price tag are pitted against each other. All this means is that either the buyer (your prospect) or you (the salesman) eventually will compromise. Result: Agreement on what it will cost your prospect to gain possession of what you have to sell.

2. VALUE.—This has strong selling power. It has persuasive power. In this, you place the worth of your product to your prospect above price consideration. What will it mean to him if he gains possession of what you have to sell? How will he benefit? That's the key to solving this price-squeeze situation.

3. CHEAPNESS.—Even the most determined price-squeeze prospect will resent it if you call him "cheap." Cheapness means a price which is below standard price. A price too low is bound to cut into the structure of what you have to sell. It has to be cheapened. In fact, or by implication, cheapness depresses the market value of a product, or of a service. Cheapness is lacking in enduring sales power.

4. DEARNESS.—This has within it a prestige factor. Prestige has HARD SELL power in a price squeeze. Dearness means that what you have for sale is, in fact, expensive. Your prospect may say, "It's too dear for my blood." But, is it really too dear? Dearness has been loosely used to imply "too rich for anybody's blood." Dearness, however, is a comparative term. It encompasses both PRICE and VALUE. It rises above CHEAPNESS. Dearness can also have potent selling power. Often it appeals to vanity. It can appeal to those who want the very best. You can strip dearness of its sales-killing power in a price squeeze. You can do this by building up dearness as something rich and desirable. You picture it as something envied by others. You can sell dearness against cheapness with the SECRET POWER IN THE HARD SELL.

To turn a price squeeze into a bonanza, you draw upon your imagination and your courage.

In a revealing case of record, the prospect was a retail dealer. He haggled for a lower price. The salesman countered with evidence of the worth of his product. "It strikes me that this is the type of quality goods your trade is looking for," the salesman said with an attitude of sureness to the dealer. "People here tell me that this is a quality house. I'm sure that a good percentage of those people would be disappointed if you offered them anything cheap in quality. Your store has a quality look. I'm right, am I not? This is a quality house, isn't it? Why don't we keep it that way and build up volume on that basis? It's more profitable, you know."

With that vanity appeal, the salesman drew attention to various pieces in his line. "Here is something rich and beautiful. Doesn't this look like quality? Feel it! Doesn't it blend with the personality of your store? Your friends are bound to be impressed by the dignity and good taste of this merchandise. They'll want it. They'll buy it. And, here's the point that will interest you most: The mark-up is mighty comfortable for you. This is a quality, profit line. You'll notice, as other merchants have noticed, that this line soon becomes a conversation topic in town. The house I represent has built up a wide clientele among people like yourself who appreciate real quality, real value, rather than cheapness."

In the sports field, the ski has become a "royal" product. Those in the know tell us that the individual outlay for ski gear and clothing is in the neighborhood of $300 and up. Quality is in demand. If we are selling to sports minded prospects, we might expect to get caught in a price squeeze. However, the ski has hopped onto the price escalator. Those who enjoy life at ski resorts are prestige minded. They want to be outfitted well. Nothing cheap. They want the maximum in safety. Ski gear must be very good. This, then, is "class" business. *Secrets of the Hard Sell* remind us to glorify the price tag. Be proud of a good selling figure. If this is sound in selling skis, then why shouldn't it be just as sound in selling other merchandise? People do want and will pay for something good. The first step to cash in on this market is to SELL THE IDEA with *Secrets of the Hard Sell.*

The Principle: Don't back away from a price squeeze. Turn it into a bonanza with *Secrets of the Hard Sell.*

Tested Ways of Enticing Prospects to Ignore the Cost

The next time one of your prospects applies the price squeeze turn the tables on him. Become persuasive. Tempt him. Offer him benefits to be derived from buying your product. This diverts his attention from cost. Aim at your prospect's five senses. Note how each of the following senses is alive with selling power:

SIGHT.—Make your proposal vivid. Let your prospect see the beneficial possibilities. Let him see how he can satisfy his self-interest by buying what you have to sell. A vivid, enticing presentation will do the trick. Cost then becomes incidental, often ignored altogether.

TOUCH.—Ask your prospect to feel your product. You may have something he will "love to touch." Softness, smoothness, richness all gain selling power through the sense of touch coupled with the sense of sight. It's difficult, if not impossible, for your prospect to feel the price. Why dwell on it?

HEARING.—Through the ears you capture your prospect's interest. He hears your enticing story of how your product can fit into his way of life. You make it appealing. You make it tempting. You do this fervently so he will ignore the cost. Doing this you break through the price squeeze.

SMELL.—If your product has fragrance, that is in your favor in a price squeeze. Make the most of it. Let his nose help you sell your product to him. Say to him: "Smell the freshness in this product. Isn't that delightful?" Freshness, newness, fragrance are all potent in selling against a price squeeze.

TASTE.—"Taste this. Isn't it delicious?" Now you're tempting your prospect. Your prospect tastes. He smacks his lips. He agrees with you that your product is "great." When he does, down goes the price-squeeze sales barrier. The sense of taste has overwhelmed price fixation. Your product was so delicious that cost was ignored.

Use of the senses is effective in meeting price objections. However, there are also other ways. When the prospect declares that your price is out of line, ask him, "Why?" This often stumps your prospect. You follow through. You show him how packed-in value in your product makes it a superior buy. You show him why your price is in line. You suggest that there will always be those who will make a cheaper product. You ask him: "You don't enjoy cheapness, do you?" You continue: "Isn't it true that we get about what we pay for? Our factories have produced, and we have sold, about 30 million dollars worth of this same item at the same price I am offering it to you. With such a volume the price must be right. Wouldn't someone have proved that our price was out of line, if it was? But, they haven't. Here's the reason. Our purpose is to keep the price as low as possible consistent with sustaining top quality. We just do not cut down on quality. Doesn't that policy make sense to you?"

When someone tightens the price squeeze on you, do this: Explore every possibility of interest which can overshadow price interest. Here are six suggested areas of interest for such exploration:

1. LUXURY.—Isn't there something luxurious about your product? Search for the luxury element. You'll find it. Luxury interests most of us. Your product has features that suggest richness, softness, smoothness, captivating beauty, distinctiveness, or even toughness. These may be classed as luxury features. And, there are others. The point is: Glorify luxury by imaginative presentation. Get worked up over color, design, quality, etc. In that way you induce your prospect to see it as you see it. You induce your prospect to buy with price only incidental in importance. The luxury angle is warm in persuasive quality. It has a tendency to divert your prospect's attention away from his price fixation.

2. DISTINCTIVENESS.—Your price-squeeze prospect may be fashion-conscious. Distinctiveness will get to him. It will turn him on. Distinctiveness pulls in business for fine dining places. This isn't because the price is low. Far from it. It's because that dining place is distinctive. Now look at your product. Isn't there something distinctive about it? There must be. Use it! Glorify it! Distinctiveness is a powerful weapon for combating a price squeeze. Use it!

3. SECURITY.—This gets close to self-interest nerve centers. Your price-squeezing prospect will yield on price if you bear down on his personal security. Those who sell insurance, investments, vaults in which to store valuables, and such things make much ado about security. It's a sure-fire selling weapon when aimed properly. How about your product? How about you? Are you security con-

scious? You can cash in on security with imaginative HARD SELLING.

4. SAFETY.—Play it safe. Self-preservation has selling appeal. The HARD SELL automobile salesman capitalizes on safety features of his car. Automobile salesmen are vulnerable to the price squeeze. But, with a "safer" car he has a special appeal. Personal safety carries a sales wallop. It often turns a price squeeze into a bonanza. Safety, luxury, distinctiveness, plus fun in driving, add up to an enticing combination in a price squeeze. They are all related to *Secrets of the Hard Sell*.

5. ENJOYMENT.—This is the self-satisfaction punch. It drives sales records up and up. Even the most fanatical price-squeezing prospect wants to get fun out of life. Show him how and he'll buy. Self-satisfaction is closely linked to self-interest. By playing on his self-interest and his self-satisfaction you can make him pliable.

6. GAIN.—Your price-squeezing prospect is actually fishing for personal gain. You can switch the approach and turn this desire into personal gain for yourself. Show him how he can make money by buying what you have to sell. Show him how he can benefit in other ways by buying what you have to sell. Already your price-squeezing prospect is profit-conscious. Your angle is to convince him that he can gain more by buying than by price wrangling. This is a tested SECRET OF THE HARD SELL for thawing the ice in a stubborn price squeeze.

The Principle: To combat a price-squeeze counter with a powerful self-interest appeal. Tell your prospect, show your prospect, convince your prospect that your proposal has more personal benefits for him than he could possibly enjoy by buying a cheap product.

Secrets of Landing Big Tag Accounts by Making Profit More Persuasive Than Price

A home furnishings dealer in a thriving western city was a much-sought-after account. He was known among salesmen as a tough buyer. He especially put bedding salesmen in a price squeeze. Price was his weapon. He wielded it with a heavy hand. Many salesmen who called on him showed timidity. They talked price. So did he. Then a new face showed up in the territory. This salesman took on the tough buyer in a different way. He began SELLING UP to that tough dealer. He broke the ice-crust by ignoring the dealer's fanaticism for price-bartering. "Our line is a quality line," he told the dealer at the outset. "It's a profit-making line." This had a warm appeal to the tough fellow. Momentarily he was disarmed. Profit was something salesmen hadn't been talking about. The new salesman held on to that dealer's interest. He showed him how his mattresses were put together. He never mentioned price. He showed how his mattresses had been designed for years of sleep comfort. He came up with endorsements of his line from other profit-making dealers. One of these dealers had written: "This line is outselling lower-priced lines in our store. We get no complaints about this line. Users of these mattresses send their friends to see us. The number of referral customers continues to increase. With us, this is our leader line. It is our most profitable line."

Here was a tough, "big tag" account that responded to profit-making. That buyer forgot about price-squeezing. Low price has a "think little" appeal. On the other hand, the THINK BIG appeal has selling punch. The secret in this situation is to show your price-haggling prospect how he can make dollars instead of how he can save pennies. Profit-hungry prospects are more responsive than penny pinchers.

Case records show that volume goes up faster with profit-wise customers. When this happens, both dealer and salesman prosper. Both are talking the same language—more value for the customer's dollar. This approach takes hold. And, why not? The dealer and the salesman are both in the SELLING business. Saving becomes incidental.

Try these six tested inducements that have broken price squeezes for other salesmen using the magic power in *Secrets of the Hard Sell:*

1. PROFIT.—Glorify the possibilities for making more money. Blot out the temptation to save a little.

2. PRESTIGE.—Tempt your prospect. Create an irresistible desire to possess. Make it irresistible by HARD SELL presentation and sustained persuasion. Glorify your product. Dress it up as a prestige-builder. Low price lacks this HARD SELL PRESTIGE appeal.

3. COMFORT.—It's amazing what people will do to enjoy rest, to relax, to find solid comfort. Sell comfort and you make a HARD SELL bid with dynamic persuasive power. Sell quality with a HARD SELL drive behind it and you're on your way to cracking the ice on any price squeeze.

4. FUN.—Have fun making money? What's cockeyed about that? Pleasure has an ever-widening market. If your line is made for fun, turn it into soaring profits with a fun-producing price. Big tag dealers in pleasure merchandise build profit volume on pleasure possibilities. The secret of selling to these dealers is this: (a) Present evidence of profit-making. (b) Show how your line offers more for the money; how it can increase profits for your prospect. (c) THINK BIG. Sell the idea of "more for the money." These three pitches are more persuasive than low price. Sell the idea of SPENDING FOR PROFIT. It's the secret of breaking a price squeeze.

5. PRIDE.—This is a double-edged sword. Jack up your prospect's pride. Glamorize your product. Glamorize pride of ownership. Capitalize on envy. "Your friends will envy you when you step out in this," has persuasive appeal. It implies that your prospect can afford the best. Pride of ownership, plus the satisfaction of generating envy, have HARD SELL possibilities for breaking the price squeeze.

6. LONG LIFE.—Durability and style are angles for selling quality shoes. In the eyes of the buyer they're worth more. An automobile salesman uses service department records as a selling tool. He sells durability—long life. "Look," he says, putting his finger on the service record, "this man drives 1,500 miles a month. He drives a car just like this one. Notice the way it holds up. This car has long life. Steady, every-day pounding on the road doesn't break it down or push up its maintenance cost. You pay a little more for this car, but look at how much more you get. Here's a convincing record of performance."

Five Steps to Drive Your "Better Buy" Message Through

To yield to the pressure of a price squeeze is defeatism. As a HARD SELL salesman, you must shrink from being a defeatist.

It just isn't done in the HARD SELL club. The HARD SELL salesman rises above the price squeeze. He picks up the tempting challenge thrown at him by his prospect. In effect, the prospect says: "I'll buy, but you'll have to come down to my price." To counter this sort of pressure, the HARD SELL salesman replies, in effect: "I'll show you a better deal. I have a much better buy for your money. What I have to propose to you will bring greater benefits to you. Any cheap substitute has no lasting quality, and a man such as you wants quality. What I propose that you should invest your hard-earned money in is something that will pay off for you for a long time. Let me show you how you can profit by taking on my product and my service."

Until you assume a positive attitude toward your price-cutting prospect you will be subject to his whims. Your sales volume will begin to grow when you quash what your prospect thinks is a tempting price squeeze.

Looking Ahead: Make note now of the following five steps for driving through with your HARD SELL, "better buy" message. These five steps are your constructive, and tested, alternative to price-cutting:

1. Steel yourself against any price squeeze. Rise above argument on price. Turn firmly, yet persuasively, to the "more-for-your-money" angle. Sell long life. Sell satisfaction. Sell more profitable resale. Sell greater public demand. Sell endurance. Sell beauty. Sell with HARD SELL ENTHUSIASM. Assume the attitude that here is the greatest value on the market today. You should buy this for your own sake. All of this sales power is wrapped up in SECRETS OF THE HARD SELL.

2. Show how little it costs to enjoy better quality, which you offer in your product. Break down your total price to a low unit price. Quote the low unit price, not the cost of the whole package. Unit prices have the persuasive low-cost sound. When you throw the gross total, or the carload price at your prospect, he may shake. This is especially true if he is a price-squeezer.

3. If you're selling a top quality product against something at a lower price point out how little it costs to enjoy the prestige of top quality. Break the price down. Show how much more value is jammed into your prestige product. Itemize to reduce the shock

effect of the total cost. Help your prospect to see it this way: "When you see how much you sacrifice by taking the cheaper product, the best really isn't over-priced, is it?"

4. Over and over again give your prospect a positive answer to his big question: "Why should I buy this at your price?" Your answer: Tell him, show him how he will benefit. Make it very plain. Simplify it. Make it easy for him to grasp the idea. List it all so he can see it—item by item, benefit by benefit, all the reasons, all the advantages. Dramatize the benefits he will gain by buying your product at your price. This is the HARD SELL with its magic power.

5. Take command of the selling situation. Slowly, steadily, subtly undermine the price squeeze technique with HARD SELL proposals to enjoy the personal benefits of a better buy. THINK BIG! HANG ON! As your prospect's price squeeze weakens he'll yield, and he'll buy.

How to Beat Down Cut-Price Competition by Dipping into Secrets of the Hard Sell

Whatever you are selling you can sell more by becoming RESTLESSLY CREATIVE. To do this, you turn on your imagination. You draw upon past failures and successes. You picture difficult people yielding to your persuasive selling. You picture tractable people increasing their volume purchases. You reach a never-rest period.

This spirit within you causes you to visualize such accomplishments. It gives you fresh ideas. You're not hopped up in doing this. RESTLESS CREATIVITY is the No. 1 SECRET OF THE HARD SELL. We discussed the sales-producing power of this No. 1 Secret in Chapter 1. We can put it to work beating down price competition. Here are the keys to unlock the power of HARD SELL SECRETS which enable you to rise above cut-price competition:

1. PRODUCT GLORIFICATION.—This is creative selling. Make the most of your line. Magnify every desirable feature of your product. One by one glorify these features. Give them radiance. Give them grandeur. Give them super-strength. Give them

utility. Make them wanted. This is HARD SELL with its magic power. It can even swing some price-squeeze experts away from their objective.

2. SIDE-STEPPING PRICE WITH A PURPOSE.—Persuasively skirt the price issue to free yourself from a price squeeze. Your hard-sell alternative:

(a) SELL QUALITY.

(b) SELL BEAUTY.

(c) SELL ENDURANCE.

(d) SELL SAFETY.

(e) SELL SECURITY.

(f) SELL DESIRABILITY.

(g) SELL PRESTIGE-BUILDING QUALITY to the point of capitalizing on envy.

Price comparison only draws attention to price. It strengthens the price squeeze. It sucks you deeper into the mire of price-cutting. To develop sales volume on a solid, constructive, profitable basis, SELL THE IDEA OF MORE FOR THE MONEY. Show more. Tell less. Demonstrate how the features of your product will yield benefits and profits to the buyer. Back it all with facts.

3. INVOLVEMENT.—To avoid a price squeeze, draw your prospect into the selling process. I observed a wholesale fabric salesman close volume business by inviting his prospect to test the textile strength of some new cloth. The test was so interesting to the dealer that price was not mentioned.

An automobile salesman closed a sale to a woman who had just completed driver instruction and received her driver's license. She was at the wheel of the car with the salesman at her side. The ease of operation of the car amazed her. "I want this car," she said gleefully. No price squeeze there.

A piano and organ salesman writes a flattering amount of business. He seats his prospect at an instrument, persuades her (or him) to play. Whether they know a musical note or not doesn't matter. That salesman has a method by which amateurs squeeze music out of either an organ or a piano. The result: A two-pronged sale. An organ or a piano is sold plus a course of private instruction in the firm's studio. All this without a price squeeze. At the close, the salesman points out the "small monthly payments" that take care of it all. In this way he sidesteps the price squeeze. The sale is complete before he gets to the price.

Salesmen who prove the comfort qualities of shoes sell more shoes. They get the shoes on the prospect's feet before they talk about comfort. Then they talk about style. They show the built-in quality of the shoe. The prospect stands up. "How's that for comfort?" The prospect makes his commitment. He buys with no price haggling.

A home appliance salesman outsells most price-cutting competitors because he gets his prospects interested in the appliance, not in the price. He gets the prospect involved in the selling process. I heard him invite a housewife to pull out the trays from the refrigerator. He encouraged her to be free to examine the appliance in her own way. She bought without discussing the price. She bought because that salesman got her involved with features that were important to her. The more she "played" with that refrigerator the less price-conscious she became.

How Secret Power in the Hard Sell Quiz Uncovers Soft Spots in the Armor of Tough Prospects

Before tackling known price-squeeze prospects take time out to do the "mirror trick." Look in that mirror for several minutes and ask that fellow you see reflected in that mirror a few questions such as:

(a) Do I firmly believe that I have the best deal available in my line to offer to my prospects?

(b) Do I believe that the price of my product is O.K.?

(c) Can I conscientiously defend the price of my product and sell with HARD SELL vigor against any price squeeze?

(d) Am I enthusiastic about the benefits my prospects can expect by buying from me?

(e) Is price my hangup? Does a price squeeze or price competition cool my enthusiasm?

The foregoing five-point quiz has its own SECRET POWER. It may reveal soft spots in your own HARD SELL ARMOR. In that case, you have corrective work to do.

The SECRET POWER in a HARD SELL quiz directed at your prospects often reveals soft spots in their sales-resisting armor. In a price squeeze this is of great value to you. You might test your next price-conscious prospect's sales-resisting armor with the following questions:

(a) Why do you think our price is too high? (The reply should tip you off on how best to get through to that prospect.)

(b) Why do you suppose this product is outselling all competition? Does that seem to support the idea that it is overpriced? (This should reveal more about your prospect's viewpoint as a clue to what your next move should be.)

(c) Which color among these samples do you prefer? (This question often reveals that your prospect is responding to your sales drive. He (or she) is, at least, willing to make a choice.)

(d) What features of this product will have the widest appeal with your customers? (The reply to this question may conceivably open the gate so you can enter with a HARD SELL presentation under full power.)

I have used the HARD SELL QUIZ as a selling tool. I have seen how productive it has been for other salesmen with high production records. Questions lead to discussion. It's a method of penetrating the sales-resisting armor of even the most fanatical price-squeezers. Questions that stimulate discussion get buyer and salesman on common ground.

The sales manager of a merchandising syndicate with far-flung operations made this observation:

"Too many salesmen are timid about asking questions. A certain amount of backbone is required in all phases of selling. The quiz is one phase. Some of our best producing salesmen use well-conceived questions as their opening wedge with new prospects. They get acquainted by quizzing. These same salesmen stiffen up and smile if a price-squeezing prospect lets loose with cut-price pressure. The timid ones back away. The bold ones, who are the producers, make a price squeeze a signal for harder selling.

"One of our men lays it on the line this way: 'Dealing with us you can be sure that nobody ever gets a better price than you get. Our policy is easy to understand. We close each order on company terms and at company prices. There are no strings attached to our orders. We are known in the market as a one-price house with one kind of service—TOPS. I'm sure you'll enjoy doing business with us. We will try to win your complete confidence. I feel sure that we'll do more business with you because you'll begin making more money with our line. In that way both of us profit.'

"I think that salesman has the answer to the price-squeeze problem. His customers know exactly where he stands on the price question. After a while they begin to believe in our one-price policy. That salesman of ours, and others in our team, do well in building sales volume against price squeezes."

An industrial machinery salesman I met pulls out his order book and lays it on the table as soon as his prospect tries to launch a price squeeze. He told me that this practice disturbed one of his prospects. "I'm not ready for that yet," the prospect flared at the salesman. "I know," the salesman replied pleasantly. "So, let's get down to seeing just what we can do to improve your plant operation to give you greater profit returns." The prospect agreed. Ten days later that salesman signed up that prospect on an order for about $31,000 worth of equipment with no price haggling. The salesman succeeded in leaving the door wide open for the possible sale of additional equipment when remodeling plans were complete.

Principle: Even in a price squeeze never doubt that you are going to land the business. The toughest price-squeeze buyers respect firmness and honesty.

10

Developing Hard Sell Power from "Impossible" Situations

The 5-point principle of developing hard sell power:

1. Motivate yourself.
2. Set up attainable targets.
3. Go after specific objectives.
4. Know what you want and why.
5. Define how you propose to get what you want.

George Melvy became a table topic in the Commerce Club. George had knocked over a most desirable account. That account had tempted scores of other salesmen. Now they were asking: "How come that George got through to that tough buyer?" And, "How come that George did what we couldn't do? We've been pecking at that account for a long time. Do you suppose it was guts or just plain luck?"

George's associates were eager to dig out his success secret. Most of those envious salesmen had tackled that "impossible" account. One by one they had given it up as an "impossible" situation.

George took a more positive view of the problem. He relied on BOLD SELLING. He gave no thought to surrendering. While his associates, including his competitors, wrote off the account, George grabbed his brief case and went after it. He mustered HARD SELL power to sell to that hard-to-convince buyer. He ran a blockade which that buyer had set up for timid salesmen. By constant probing, George found a way to penetrate that barrier. He worked all angles, from delivery men to secretaries and receptionists. By persistence he got in. He then stood face to face with that "unapproachable" prospect. He wasn't a bad guy after all. George had found that the door to that buyer's inner office was well guarded. He also discovered that it could be opened by resourcefulness. When he got in George sold his idea to that tough prospect with HARD SELL conviction. He came out of that "impossible" situation with a substantial order instead of an excuse. He also left that heavily guarded door ajar. He wanted to come back later and sell again. He had experienced what guts and HARD SELL power can do in strongly motivated selling.

In a sales conference of a competitive firm the obvious question was aked: "What was George's secret?"

One of George's more intimate competitive salesmen attended that meeting. He put it this way:

(a) George knew WHERE he was going.
(b) He knew HOW he would get there.
(c) He knew WHY he was going there.
(d) He knew WHAT he proposed to do when he got there.

MOTIVATION was the basic SECRET of George's success in landing that "impossible" account.

The ultimate of HARD SELL MOTIVATION requires guts. It's the essence of bold selling.

The secret of why George's associates failed to get through to the hard-to-get-at prospect while George succeeded is pertinent:

Those who failed had been *hard-selling themselves out of the sale*. The prospect's reputation for being tough had infected them with gutless defeatism. They became fearful. They gave up after feeble attempts to penetrate a formidable sales barrier. When rebuffed they backed away. In lieu of returning to their offices with complete orders, they returned with cooked up excuses.

What about George? He took a look, perhaps several looks, at that same account. He decided the account could be sold. So he came up with this solution to his problem: (a) He convinced himself that he had sufficient guts to break through the barriers set up by that prospect. (b) He convinced himself that once inside he could and he would sell to that prospect. (c) He developed a well-ordered plan to achieve his purpose. As George saw it nothing less than the *Secrets of the Hard Sell* would do the job. So, he set up the following must-do objectives:

1. Develop sufficient guts to tackle this "impossible" situation with a sales-producing HARD SELL plan.
2. Muster maximum hard sell power to convert this "impossible" account into a profitable account.
3. Prepare to open with HARD SELL at the moment of contact with the "impossible" prospect.
4. Cool that cantankerous prospect by HARD SELL PERSUASION.
5. Make a "live," eager prospect out of him with dynamic presentations.
6. Lay the foundation for developing that "impossible" prospect into a long-time customer.
7. Combat fear of either the tough prospect or of failure.
8. Think only of success. Think only of selling. Recognize that guts can develop the required HARD SELL power.

The Principle: Motivate yourself!

How the Secret Power of the Hard Sell Knocks Out Fear

In one year, a young salesman climbed from a poor beginning to top the staff in sales. The driving force which boosted that young man into the five-figure class was perserverance, guts and *Secrets of the Hard Sell*.

That salesman's line was the most competitive in the field. It involved expenditures of thousands of dollars by those who bought the idea. High risks were involved. That salesman was selling sales-promoting advertising services of various kinds. Those services stood up or fell down on their merits and on how they were used. To sell his "product" that salesman had to get fear out of his system. His line required bold selling. This he discovered early in his career. He became convinced that timidity was out if he hoped to succeed. He told me that at the outset he drew up the following guidelines for himself:

No. 1.—TRAIN YOURSELF TO MAKE DECISIONS. Avoid dangling problems. Make firm, totally positive decisions. Not half-way compromising decisions. The mere act of deciding on something generates courage. Indecision breeds fearfulness. Decision stimulates thinking. Indecision invites the other person to decide for you. This weakens you. If you surrender to your prospect, you allow him to decide. Invariably, such a decision by a prospect will be against you. In selling, the decision will be a blunt "no" or, at best, an excuse for not buying at that time. When a sale is at stake, your objective must constantly be to persuade your prospect to say "yes."

No. 2.—HAVE FAITH. Believe in something. Cultivate an unshakable belief that YOU CAN SELL to the toughest prospect on your list. Cultivate an unshakable belief that you can build your line into high volume production. One master of the HARD SELL worked by a simple credo to build high volume sales. Here is that credo: "Live just so, but don't slip into an apologetic rut."

No. 3.—DOUBT IS THE SECRET SALES-KILLER. Self-doubting is a destroyer. Rise above it. You're no better than you think you are. Make your slogan, "CAN DO." Whimperings of the weak produce few if any sales. Guard against these doubt signals: "I wonder if I'm up to this challenge. I wonder if this will sell. I wonder if that prospect will give me a break." Sales volume isn't built on a foundation of such doubts. The alternative attitude is to encourage the foes of doubt. Make every day a full day of HARD SELL contacts with prospective buyers. Take on the tough ones with eagerness and guts. The magic power of one productive HARD SELL day is well known to top-bracket producers. When in doubt, they don't sit in the club and sip highballs. They get on their feet and begin knocking on doors. In this way they take command over their doubts. Their bold selling attitude is a natural for success. It kills doubt and fear as a fly-swatter kills flies.

In diplomacy, John Quincy Adams demonstrated that he was a MASTER OF THE HARD SELL. He sneered at fear. He left the following thought for us. Even those of us who sell can profit by this bit of Adams' wisdom: "Courage and perseverance have a magical talisman, before which difficulties disappear and obstacles vanish into air."

In today's language of the market place, guts and perseverance are the driving forces that achieve HARD SELL SUCCESS.

Of course, there is a risk involved in BOLD SELLING. But, fear magnifies any risk until the risk becomes a real danger. Courage cuts risk down to size and tramples on it. Developing courage is an exercise in crushing fear. Actually, it is your primary weapon for dislodging ghosts. You know, of course, that when fear dominates your selling day, ghosts have put down their roots in your private soil. THE SECRET OF THE HARD SELL roots out those ghosts. That power knocks out fear. It turns timidity around and kicks it out of your way. Hard sell salesmen in every line on the market at some time or other must attack ghosts that threaten to haunt them. With the allied selling strength of *Secrets of the Hard Sell,* those salesmen plunge ahead to success by frightening away the ghosts that would have frightened them.

Pete McCord was a good salesman. His associates looked up to him. They admired his record and also his guts in selling. He went after the seemingly "impossible" prospects. He rose above the peddler class. He was, in fact, a disciple of BOLD SELLING. Other salesmen and sales executives sought him out. They wanted to know more about his secret. I knew this man when he was a timid soul. I asked him how he beat down that handicap. He replied with that sureness of purpose which comes when doubt is dispelled:

> I first had to get motivated. I had to dedicate myself to a worthwhile purpose. I had to learn how to become brave in dealing with people. I became motivated by observing how fright often lost sales for otherwise good men. I became motivated by observing how other men landed sales by guts, by

bold selling and by sound thinking. I saw those men become confident. I saw how creative selling gave many of them guts. I saw one man who had once been afraid but who now was a great showman in selling. If anything could be animated that man would animate it. And, he would sell it. Prospects had a hard time resisting buying from that man.

Then I saw timid souls, such as I had been. I saw them stand back and stare when a prospect barked at them. It soon dawned on me that it was the salesman with guts who was setting sales records. One of those hard-selling men got hot and bothered about what he planned to present to a prospect. Suddenly an idea flashed into his mind. He went in boldly and rapped on that prospect's door. When he was admitted, he went into action at once. He related his product to the interests of his prospect. He demonstrated how the prospect could benefit by buying what he had to sell. Once he had aroused the slightest interest that salesman had the guts to build on that interest. He stayed with his prospect. He concentrated on the prospect's self interest. By HARD SELL persistence he eventually got the "yes" answer he was after. His SECRET: He maintained momentum in hard selling until the prospect initialed the order.

Great salesmen are self-made. They get that way because they are headed in one direction: AHEAD. They do this by BOLD SELLING. They do this by mastering *Secrets of the Hard Sell*. In every selling situation they take charge. By activating those tested secrets of successful selling, they frighten away the ghosts of fear. They capitalize on all sorts of resistance. They apply the principles of the HARD SELL. They hammer away to get business. This is their method of making war on fear. ALL this eventually pays off for them. Why? Because the MAGIC OF THE SECRET POWER OF THE HARD SELL is released to create sales for them.

How to Close Tough Sales by Courageous Selling

The essence of the SECRET OF CLOSING SALES, including the tough ones, is recorded in the best-selling book of all time.

Here it is: *"Ask,* and it shall be given you; *seek* and ye shall find; *knock* and it shall be opened unto you."—Luke 11:9.

The key to closing is this: ASK. But, first spadework must be done. Your prospect has set up obstacles. These obstacles are intended to prevent you from selling. You must topple these obstacles, one by one, if you are to close the sale. The HARD SELL will do this. These obstacles are mainly your prospect's excuses. We have labeled those excuses as obstacles. Perhaps "obstacle" sounds more formidable to us. Perhaps we think that crushing an "obstacle" requires more heroic measures than crushing an "excuse." Perhaps we are also kidding ourselves. When we apply the HARD SELL to close a sale, we will be introduced to an assortment of excuses. At that point we will discover whether we are late in asking for the order. Nevertheless, we must cut through the barrier. We must close or we cannot sell. That's elementary. Thus, closing becomes our ultimate objective in selling.

How, then, do we go about closing? I put that question to several record-breaking salesmen. I asked them *when* and *how* they moved in to close a sale. From their replies I gleaned the following tips on closing:

1. HAVE COURAGE to ask for the order.
2. HAVE COURAGE TO ASK FOR THE ORDER EARLY, OFTEN . . . never relenting.
3. HAVE COURAGE TO SUMMARIZE when your sales drive seems to be losing persuasive power.
4. HAVE COURAGE TO POINT OUT the benefits of buying now.
5. HAVE COURAGE TO STRESS the possibility of losing benefits if buying is delayed.
6. HAVE COURAGE TO REPEATEDLY TRY TO CLOSE.
7. HAVE COURAGE TO PERSUADE your prospect to declare his choice of two or three options.
8. HAVE COURAGE TO CONVERT your prospect's excuses for not buying into selling points with "buy-now" impact.

9. HAVE COURAGE TO CAPITALIZE on emotional possibilities in what you have to sell.

10. HAVE COURAGE TO DRAMATIZE your product or service.

11. HAVE COURAGE TO CONVERT buying objections into reasons for buying.

12. HAVE COURAGE TO REITERATE every sales point and re-emphasize every benefit that can accrue to your prospect by buying now.

The HARD SELL salesmen who gave me these tips were also telling me to do this:

SMILE when your prospect spars with you for advantage.

GRIN when your prospect bluntly refuses to buy. Have guts enough to carry on.

MOVE IN QUICKLY when your prospect shakes his head and says "no." Get him back on the self-interest track. He's now quite satisfied with himself. He's patting himself on the back. He thinks he has stopped you. He's about to usher you out of his office. Don't let him do it!

Frequently, a question can change the atmosphere in a situation that appears to be going against you. For instance, you might ask your prospect: "In your opinion, what is wrong with my proposal?" If he hesitates and gropes for an answer, which he probably will, reassure him in this way: "There must be something not quite right from your viewpoint. For your sake I'm very interested in what that is. If you can identify that problem for me, we probably can get together on an idea that will be beneficial to you."

I have used that technique to derail a prospect who had refused to buy. I have also succeeded in getting objecting prospects back on the track. A direct question usually exposes the frailty of most excuses offered by prospects. I have seen HARD SELL salesmen use the direct-question technique. I have also witnessed them close sales by this method. I have experienced the thrill of turning a blunt turndown into a closed sale.

Variety is the fascinating thing about exploring the vast possibilities in *Secrets of the Hard Sell*. No two cases are identical. We are dealing with people. Duplicates are rare. Because of this we strive to understand people better. The more we find out about our prospects, the better qualified we become to sell more. So we search for knowledge of a prospect's wants, his needs, his hopes, his ambitions, his resources, and his ability to buy and pay for what we have to sell. To achieve this HARD SELL objective we reach out for mastery of *Secrets of the Hard Sell*.

I have found that the most successful salesmen like people. They enjoy watching them. The tide of humanity flowing through the marketplaces fascinates those people. In the eyes and actions of people those discerning salesmen see opportunities for their own success.

When tough sales are closed, I have seen how thrilled successful salesmen become. They have met the challenge that prospects have hurled at them. They have accepted those challenges. They have capitalized on them. They found joy in overcoming resistance. Selling never becomes boring to them.

I have found that most successful salesmen are courageous. They are proud of their profession. They are proud of their products or services. They are proud of the firms they represent. PRIDE is one of the keys to their successes. Because they have pride in what they are selling, their presentations have life, enthusiasm, and persuasive quality. . . . Because they have pride in themselves, they have guts enough to tackle the toughest of the tough-to-sell situations.

I have found that most successful salesmen are enthusiastic. Their theme is to benefit those to whom they sell. They are sincere. They firmly believe they can do this. They sell more than a product. They are IDEA MERCHANTS. The magic power of accomplishment which they show is also contained in *Secrets of the Hard Sell*.

An advertising salesman I know has achieved his major successes in closing tough sales. He is a courageous, HARD SELLING man. He has a warm, enthusiastic handshake and a winning smile. He also has a fighting spirit. When the chips are down, he closes the tough ones by BOLD SELLING. On one occasion he related this to me:

> That prospect gave me a 'wet-towel-in-the-face' reception. When I think of how easily I could have lost that deal it raises goose pimples all over me. My experience with that guy

taught me that it doesn't pay to over-inflate yourself. It also taught me that ideas are more salable than merchandise. When I swung into showing that guy how my product could be used to his advantage he began to nibble at the bait. He became warm. The ice was melting. I caught the fever and kept on rolling. I was selling profits, comfort, pride of owner-ship, and beauty, plus other things associated with my prod-uct. And he bought, willingly. But, I'm still chilled because I came mighty close to killing that sale myself.

In a military sense George S. Patton was a HARD SELL salesman. He sold his men on the idea of winning battles. He taught his men what courage meant. He glorified guts. In selling, we, too, need guts to compete in today's hard-fought sales battles. General Patton said: "Discipline, pride, self-respect, self-confidence, are attributes which will make a man courageous even when he is afraid." Apply the Patton theme to selling and you have turned the spotlight on another SECRET OF THE HARD SELL.

How to Switch to the Hard Sell to Change An "Impossible" Situation

I was green as they come when I first struck out with a sample case in hand. It wasn't long until I was up against an "impossible" situation. My first commission checks gave me courage. Looking back, my income from that initial venture into selling was puny. But I had guts enough to keep going.

In time, the inevitable happened. I had targeted in on a prospect who did a volume business. My line was commercial calendars. It was a top-flight line. I was enthusiastic about it. I was sold on calendars as an advertising medium. I got all set up to go after that prospect I had set my sights on. My prospect cut me off short:

"Nobody uses calendars any more," he snorted. "They're ancient."

My spinning brain slowed down. Then I recalled that I had a literary gem in my brief case. I thought it might save the day for me. It dealt with the mission of the calendar. It contained this HARD SELL message:

"I am the calendar. . . . I hope I can help to insure for those who employ me that all important asset—your business friendship and good will."

I laid this printed card before my prospect. He read it thoroughly. Then he looked at me with a thoughtful expression on his face. "Puts a new slant on a calendar," he said.

In little more than an hour after that, I came out with an order double the size of what I had anticipated. I had gained stature with my prospect. My product had gained stature with him. I had boosted my self-confidence. In that hour I had switched away from an "impossible" situation into the HARD SELL. My first attempt at bold selling had paid off. By using selling tools that were available to me and through the magic power of HARD SELL persuasion I closed that sale.

When I first heard about HARD SELL methods, I was green in the business. I had always thought that HARD SELL meant some sort of ramrod selling. But now I know that case records reveal the magic power of *Secrets of the Hard Sell*. It is a persuasive force when used as such. At times, it soothes a prospect into buying. It has a softening, enticing effect on stubborn prospects. Note this two-point SECRET of effectively switching to the HARD SELL to change an "impossible" situation:

Point No. 1.—DON'T PUSH. People resent force. They dislike being shoved. Prospects rebel against obvious efforts to compel them to act against their will. There is a more effective way of exerting buying pressure.

Point No. 2.—Instead. . . . PULL! . . . A strong PULL is persuasive. It draws your prospect toward you. You get close to him. THE SECRET: (a) Infuse your HARD SELL presentation with MAGNETISM. (b) Sell with magnetic inducements. (c) PULL your prospect into the picture. (d) DRAW your prospect's attention to how much he has to gain by buying from you. . . . NOW! All this adds up to PULLING POWER.

When pulling power is strengthened with self-interest, it has HARD SELL effect. The active SECRET OF THE HARD SELL is pulling power.

I recall a man on whom I had never before called. He operated a large commission house. I met him on the sales floor of his main building. He was cold to my introduction. "Don't you understand, this is Saturday," he roared at me. I did not immediately reply.

He laughed boisterously. "Saturday is our big day for selling," he added. Pointing his finger at me, he said: "This is not a buying day."

I thanked him for clearing that matter up. Then I asked him: "Does Mr. Tompkins down the street both buy and sell on Saturdays?"

My prospect quickly replied: "I'm not sure. Why?" His tone was more conciliatory.

I replied: "I'm going down to talk to Mr. Tompkins. You see I represent one of the great houses in the country. It is important for us to get into this area without any delay. We didn't scratch Saturdays from our work schedule. We have an exclusive proposition. We chose you as first to consider this proposal in this area. Sorry that Saturday is an off-day for you. That puts Mr. Tompkins next on my list."

I had almost reached the exit door when my prospect yelled: "What is your deal?"

I yelled back to him: "I doubt if you'd be interested on a Saturday." By now he was almost running toward me. I added: "You must understand we set up only one dealer in an area of this size. . . ."

By that time my prospect was at my side. There was eagerness in his expression. I gave him the full HARD SELL treatment. He came down to earth in fine spirit. I had firmly switched to the HARD SELL. I had turned an "impossible" situation into a new dealership.

EXCLUSIVENESS was the magnetic idea that ignited that cold situation into a hot sales confrontation. Exclusiveness had PULL POWER. People like to be different. My prospect was proud of his merchandising leadership in that area. He wanted to stay that way. He didn't relish the idea of something new and exclusive going to his competitor down the street, even on Saturday. If you have something in your line that you can classify as unusual, try labeling it as "exclusive." There is an inducement in this if your product is *bona fidely* "exclusive." If this is the case you can build sales volume by capitalizing on its distinctiveness and its unusual qualities. This requires facts and courage. It requires guts, if you please. It also requires honesty of purpose. It requires the HARD SELL with its pulling power.

Daniel Webster demonstrated how to sell an idea. His record

sparkles with courage. He garnered votes in political campaigns. He served as Secretary of State and there he did a HARD SELL job in diplomacy. Webster had persuasive power. He had guts. Sydney Smith, a distinguished Britisher, compared Webster to a "steam engine in trousers." You and I, as salesmen, can profit by the following observation made by Smith: "A great deal of talent is lost in the world for want of a little courage. The fact is, that to do anything in the world worth doing, we must not stand back and shiver."

One of the most fiery speakers I ever heard got his audience nodding when he detected that he was losing his grip on them. By getting their heads bobbing up and down, he recaptured their interest. That up-and-down nodding was not due to drowsiness. It was a signal that they were agreeing with him. That speaker was also a salesman. Nodding was one of his SECRETS OF SWITCHING TO THE HARD SELL. That up-and-down nod amounted to saying: "Yes. That's right. I agree with you." In selling, that man worked on his prospects as he worked on an audience when he was doing public speaking. He asked questions, projected answers, and got his listeners to nod in agreement with him. At times, this required a bit of doing. But, he had the guts to get it done in his way and to his own HARD SELL advantage. He was a MASTER OF THE HARD SELL. You and I can also become masters of the HARD SELL by courageous action in "impossible" situations. He seldom pushed. He always pulled. Let's profit by doing the same.

The Principle: Each affirmative nod weakens sales resistance. When your prospect audibly says "yes" and nods agreement at the same time, you have closed the sale with another SECRET OF THE HARD SELL.

Tested Hard Sell Tips for Turning Cool Situations into Hot Ones

Zero in on the following four primary objectives for turning cool situations into hot ones:

1. TO COUNTERACT CHILLINESS IN PROSPECTS: Replace coldness with the warmth of the secret power of the HARD SELL.

2. TO COMBAT INDIFFERENCE IN PROSPECTS: Make warm presentations. Heat up your sales pitch with the fuel from *Secrets of the Hard Sell*.

3. TO CLASSIFY PROSPECTS: Hear them out. Get to know them better. Find out more about why they act and react as they do.

4. TO CAPITALIZE ON "PULL" POWER: Pull more, shove less. Draw prospects to the buying point. Capitalize on the magnetic warmth in HARD SELL "pull" power.

In almost every field of selling, *Secrets of the Hard Sell* IN ACTION come to light. Prospective buyers become convinced that they can benefit by buying. Sales are closed. But sales that are closed, without involving the self-interest of the buyer, lack permanence. Many one-time sales fall into this category. A prospect may buy because the salesman is a friend. At times, this is a sympathy sale. The buyer feels that by buying he has done his good turn for the day. On the other hand, that same prospect may buy because that salesman friend convinced him that he would profit by buying. When this happens, friendship is cemented. The buyer becomes a satisfied and enthusiastic customer. When that salesman returns, that customer is glad to receive him. The prospect looks to him as more than a friend. That salesman has qualified as a sales counselor. He has gained status. More sales are in the offing for him.

Check the following 10 tips. They include HARD SELL SECRETS that have changed "impossible" situations into closed sales. Try to relate these tips to your own situations. Innovate. Squeeze the maximum HARD SELL BENEFITS for you out of these 10 tips:

Tip No. 1.—Step into your prospect's shoes. Look at your proposal from your prospect's point of view. There is a difference, isn't there? Now, shift your presentation to his viewpoint. Show him how he can benefit. Sell HARDER with revised and revitalized HARD SELL persuasion.

Tip No. 2.—Get deeply interested in your prospect's problems. Work with him to solve those problems. Your interest can have a warming effect on the coolest prospect. When that warmth penetrates his chilled exterior you'll notice something happen. You'll see his eyes light up when you talk about how he can improve his situation. As you release HARD SELL POWER, your prospect responds to your sincere interest in his welfare. He becomes willing, even anxious to buy.

Tip No. 3.—Inflate your prospect. Make him feel like a "big shot." Talk up to him. Never down. Make him the important person in your discussion. Refrain from boasting. Let the glory be his. In this situation your prospect is, in fact, the "big shot." He'll buy if you ask him to buy. He'll buy if you have exposed him properly to the magic power in *Secrets of the Hard Sell.*

Tip No. 4.—Glorify your prospect. Keep the spotlight on him and his interests. You step into the background. Permit your prospect to have full freedom of the stage. Promote him. Dangle the prospects of profits or other benefits before him constantly. Use the full persuasive power in *Secrets of the Hard Sell.*

Tip No. 5.—Tug at your prospect's heartstrings. Search for the human interest angle. Be sincere. Never become objectionably obvious. Capitalize on emotion. It has tremendous power. Emotion has "PULL" power. Emotion has sales-building power. Develop the art of tugging at your prospect's heart strings.

Tip No. 6.—Sell ideas! Sell WHAT and HOW. Sell what your product or service can do for your prospect. Sell him on how he can profit or otherwise benefit by buying from you. Sell him on why he should buy now. Fit your product or service and its uses into your HARD SELL presentation of promised rewards for buying.

Tip No. 7.—Play on your prospect's ego. Adroitly flatter him. Butter his ego. Help him conquer his fears. Destroy his doubts. Do these things by BOLD SELLING. Do these things by perceptive selling. Reach out to your prospect. Draw him near to you. Help him muster the courage to make that firm decision which is so important to you. Help him decide to buy.

Tip No. 8.—Size up your prospect. Constantly appraise him. Has he sufficient resources with which to exploit your product at a profit to himself and to you? What is your overall estimate of your prospect? Is he frank or evasive? Is he a spender or tight-fisted? Is he argumentative or a smooth bargainer? Is he fast-moving or a dawdler? Is he imaginative and creative? Is he a success-minded climber? How does he react to profit possibilities? Do you fully trust this man? Why?

Tip No. 9.—Avoid argument. Your prospect's objections deserve respect. Tell him you're glad he made that point. Repeat his objection. This reassures you that you understand his point. Get his confirmation, too. Be sure he also understands his own objection. All this gives you time to think. It clears the air. It provides you with a fresh start on relating your selling point to his objection. You are now on your way to capitalize on his objection. No matter how hard your prospect objects, try to turn his objections into selling points. HARD SELL repetition often will cause your prospect to see it your way. For example, you might respond to his objection in this way: "I realize how easy it is to get that impression, but let me restate my point." Or, "I had the same idea about this at one time. Then I discovered a more profitable way. . . ." Or, "That certainly is sound thinking. When we look at it in this way we see even greater profit possibilities. Let me explain. . . ."

Tip No. 10.—You may be tempted to ask bluntly, "WHY?" The question may irritate some prospects. It may be difficult for your prospect to give you a logical reason why he is against buying. Use discretion. In some cases it might be better to recap the benefits possible in your proposal. This ignores the objection. This is the HARD SELL method. Your prospect may have said: "I can't afford it." Instead of asking "why?" you respond with: "Not even if this small investment will bring these benefits to you right now?" Then, with renewed HARD SELL enthusiasm you again go over the self-interest points.

Principle: In all instances keep your objective in mind. Rise above objections. Develop guts to muster HARD SELL power to overcome "impossible" situations.

Myth of Market Saturation and How to Override It by a Head-On Collision with Secrets of the Hard Sell

Even in this day of HARD SELL VICTORIES, masters of the HARD SELL hear these explanations for turning in blank sales reports:

"That market is so saturated that there is no chance to sell there. Too many dealers. They're all moaning."

"That market is gluttered with foreign cars. You can't buck that situation."

"Salesmen are starving in that territory. Good floor covering lines are not moving. The market is saturated with cheap carpet."

Excuses? You can bet your HARD SELL record on that.

Market saturation is a common excuse for not selling. But there are salesmen who ignore the myth of market saturation. They go right ahead and write up sales in volume. This happens in areas which salesmen have been warned to stay away from. Those salesmen recognize that "market saturation" is too often a bogey man. Salesmen with guts plunge in to prove that it is a myth. They override the myth. They go in with courage and the spirit to sell, even if the situation is "impossible."

Here's how the myth of saturated markets has been profitably tapped by courageous salesmen and how it can be done again, even by you and me:

1. Turn to the fundamentals of HARD SELL PROSPECTING. Pick your targets. Go after prospects who are capable of buying and benefiting by buying what you have to sell.

2. Jazz up your sales presentations. Put more HARD SELL ENTHUSIASM into your selling. Make your product come alive. Make it appear to be desirable. Make it wanted. *Secrets of the Hard Sell* will do the job for you.

3. Think success! Talk success! Believe that success is possible even in "impossible" situations. Convince your prospects that the "market saturation" bogey man is offering a fresh sales challenge to them.

I recall a typewriter salesman who had been warned that a resort town was saturated with typewriters. He was skeptical. He went in to find out. It was true. The town was saturated with antique typewriters. It wasn't an "impossible" situation as he had been forewarned. The challenge was perfectly clear to him: Replace those antiques with modern machines. He had the guts to go after that "saturated" market. First he sold his home office on supplying him with "sample" machines. His purpose: to get people involved with his product. In a few days, he had ten modern type-writers clicking away in stores and shops on a trial basis. He left these machines a day or two. This was long enough for secretaries and typists and even bosses to get interested in them. When he returned, he showed his prospects many features they had never discovered. He showed them how these gadgets worked. He showed them what these gadgets could do for them. This salesman moved steadily toward his goal. He turned trial machines into sold machines. He got more trial machines. He made more sales. He sold about $10,000 worth of them in a "saturated" market—an "impossible situation." His secret: Guts enough to tackle the "impossible." Imagination enough to make the HARD SELL a fascinating, creative venture.

The sales representative of a nationally recognized home-study school enrolled ten students by bold selling plus refreshments. He invited 20 selected prospects to be his guests at a coffee shop for coffee and doughnuts. They were college dropouts. Financial woes had kept them out of classrooms. This bold-selling salesman preached the doctrine of success via home study. His session with this group netted him 16 live prospects. On these he concentrated his fire with *Secrets of the Hard Sell*. Eventually, ten of them enrolled with him. This was imaginative, persuasive, bold salesmanship. His secret was that he had the guts to try something different. He refused to believe that the education market was saturated. He proved that it was not. He also profited.

Quite often the "market saturation" bogey man pops up in rural communities. In food, for example, a few brands may be entrenched in a limited market. In one such town, two brands of coffee had the right-of-way. Salesmen handling other brands got the "saturation" brush-off. A new salesman with a leading brand of coffee tackled that "saturated" town. He recognized that if he captured the whole market it would not be earth-shaking for the national economy. But he was eager to see if he could break through that fortress held by two competitive brands. First he sold the merchants on the idea of demonstrations. With demonstrations he drew the villagers into the act. They made the taste tests. They confirmed his HARD SELL pitch that his coffee was tops in flavor. A little free coffee, a series of demonstrations, and a liberal dose of *Secrets of the Hard Sell* and the sales barrier in that "saturated" town was broken.

Attitude can generate strong persuasive power. A positive attitude can override myths and conquer excuses in selling. One business executive made this observation: "So live each day," said Golden K. Driggs, "that you can look at the person in the mirror at the end of the day and say: 'Well done. . . . we'll do even better tomorrow.' "

You can enjoy the fruits of conquering "impossible" situations. You can do this by applying this A, B, C formula to selling:

(a) Develop guts enough to cut yourself loose from what may be hindering you and sell with all your HARD SELL POWER.

(b) Break through mythical, bogey man barriers ·y BOLD SELLING.

(c) Utilize all *Secrets of the Hard Sell* and prove lːat success is possible, never "impossible."

11

Secrets of the Hard Sell that Turn Insults into Victory

The sale of burial plots became a HARD SELL CHAL-LENGE for a salesman I knew. It was a new field for him. As he got into the field he became deeply involved in developing a "memorial park."

In this venture, that salesman learned to endure insults. He became accustomed to sales resistance. At times, this resistance was dished up as an insult. At the outset, a prime prospect insulted him. He became abusive. He ridiculed the salesman for being identified with cemetery promotion. "He was sour on the whole idea," the salesman said. "When that fellow blew his top my first inclination was to run. Instead I hung on. I let him talk himself out. In time he gasped to me: 'You can't really be serious about putting over this idiotic idea?' That outburst tipped me off that I was on my way to victory. He had now opened the gate. I could now show him and tell him what this idiotic idea was all about. I had a large map of the project. This detailed map was prepared by engineers. It lacked the appealing beauty I needed. But, I had an artist's conception of what our memorial park would look like. This was more spectacular. It would do the trick for me. I opened up on that man who had insulted me. I began by selling beauty to him instead of boundary lines. I revealed to him a number of businessmen of stature in the community who were reserving family plots. They were buying 'before need.' I told him how they had decided that it was unfair of them to leave such burdens to their wives to bear if tragedy should strike without warning. Not once did my obstinate prospect challenge my presentation on that point. He bought. This led into the investment possibilities. This was my secondary objective. I had first wanted him to become directly involved. With that accomplished, he was ripe for becoming a share holder in the company."

In the whole selling process, that salesman leveled a dual sales appeal on his prospect. One side to cut down his resistance to buying burial plots. The other had dollar appeal. He persuaded his prospect to profit by investing in shares in the project.

"Facts subdued my insolent prospect," the victorious salesman told me. "I had profited by keeping my mouth shut. I had profited by giving him plenty of rope and freedom to rave. His own raving played a part in self-selling him on my project. The result proved it. He willingly bought a choice family plot. He also bought a substantial block of stock in the deal. He had become a factor in what he had so rudely condemned."

Patience was the basic SECRET of how that salesman turned insolence into victory. As Thomas Jefferson once put it: "When angry count ten before you speak; if very angry, a hundred."

At times we encounter insolent prospects. This happens regardless of what we are selling. Insults can make us angry. But, anger doesn't close sales. Anger is a liability. Anger lacks that magic power we find in HARD SELL PERSUASION.

Seneca, the Roman philosopher, had an antidote for the poison of anger. It was "delay." Will Rogers had his own idea about "losing our heads." He said: "People who fly into a rage always make a bad landing." But, both Seneca and Will Rogers had similar ideas about what to do when provoked, as we are by an insult. Both said: "Hold your temper." It's the HARD SELL thing to do. In fact, it's another SECRET OF THE HARD SELL.

Had my friend who was promoting a memorial park blown up when his first prime prospect insulted him, he would have lost a friend and probably would have lost two substantial sales—(1) a family burial plot, and (2) a hunk of stock in the company.

We do have a problem when we are stung by an insult. Smarting under the sting, we naturally want to retaliate. But, that doesn't solve our selling problem. Retaliation will gain no sales for us. The problem is this: How can I convert an insult into a sale? It's that simple. Here's a three-point solution to that problem:

1. Give your insolent prospect credit for being sincere.
2. Grant that your insolent prospect has a reason for being insolent.
3. Assume that he probably has three targets in mind: (a) The firm you represent; (b) the product you sell; (c) yourself.

The prospect who hurls insults is often trying to lay down a smoke screen. He feels stronger when he becomes insolent. Much of this is self-defeating. Cutting a salesman down to size by insulting him pays no dividends to the insolent prospect. In time he becomes aware of this.

We find that an insolent man or woman is generally a "show off." For instance, I was in a retail store one day when a salesman came in. I overheard the merchant who ran the place whisper to another man near him. "Watch! I'll show you how to get rid of peddlers like that fellow coming toward us." When the salesman introduced himself, the manager tightened up and replied: "You must be one of those peddlers who never quite gets smart enough to understand that we don't buy on Saturday. This is our big selling day."

While the merchant was having his fun the salesman said nothing. Finally he extended his hand, picked up his sample case and headed for the door. Before making his exit he put down his sample case and pulled a notebook from his pocket. The insolent merchant was watching every move. The salesman went back to the merchant. "I have here the name of Mr. _____. I am sure you can tell me where he does business." Immediately the "show off" came down to earth. "He's one block north of here and across the street." The salesman thanked him, again picked up his bag and started toward the door. The merchant shouted: "Just a minute. What did you want to see him about?" "I expect to show him our line. He has been highly recommended to us, as you were." The merchant then suggested: "Maybe I could take a few minutes for you right now." The salesman thanked him but said his line was so important that it would require much more than a few minutes to evaluate it properly. He added: "I understand Mr. _____ does business on Saturday."

On Monday that salesman returned. The "show off" had changed his mood. He was eager to find out what luck the salesman had with the other merchant down the street. The salesman let him guess. The fire in the insolent merchant had gone out. This time he bought. In months to come, that salesman made it a point to call on that merchant on Saturdays whenever his schedule permitted. By HARD SELL magic he had changed Saturdays into buying days for that prospect. The salesman had placed that prospect's self-interest on the block and thus had gained in stature himself. He had profited by the dollar power in a quick trip from insults to victory via *Secrets of the Hard Sell*.

When the Buyer Turns Against You, Turn on the Secret Power of the Hard Sell

An alert sales promotion specialist seized opportunities to shake off discouragement. When prospects turned against him, he made buyers out of them. He was able to do this because he understood why they acted as they did. He had insight into human nature. "Impossible," did you say? More and more salesmen are doing this. That specialty salesman did it mainly by self-discipline. He learned something from every prospect who turned against him. He became a student of human motives. He was constantly intrigued by two questions:

1. WHY DO SOME OF MY PROSPECT'S BUY?
2. WHY DO SOME OF MY PROSPECT'S FREEZE UP and turn away from me?

That salesman told me that he had taught himself to dig out the motives of his prospects. "I sincerely believe," he said, "that every prospect who turns me down has a good reason for doing so. It is up to me to find out what that reason is. How else could I combat it? I also believe that those who buy from me have a reason for doing so. I also believe that it is up to me to find out what that reason is."

There are two ways for us to get at motives for buying and for not buying. First, let us re-examine the problem: (a) Why did that last prospect buy from me? (b) Why did the one before him freeze up? We have at least two ways by which to find the answers. Note that each question has a WHY angle:

1. WHY WAS I SO HOT?—This question aims at the heart of self-evaluation. You size up your successful sales presentations. Doing this you can better understand why your prospect reacted favorably. Your prospect probably could not tell you what persuaded him to buy. But you can determine why you became so persuasive. To do this you re-examine each sales pitch you made. You pick your presentations to pieces. You recall reactions of your prospects. The power thrusts you made in your presentations come back to you. You feel them again. Your weakest moments show up in your self-examination. You see how they could have strengthened and *why* they failed.

2. WHY DID MY PROSPECT FREEZE?—This is a direct challenge to you to evaluate yourself honestly. It places the blame for failure on you. Why do this? Because your prospect turned his back on you. He had a reason. He froze. *Why?* It's time to take stock of yourself. It's time to recognize that your prospect is still a live one. Don't scratch him off your list. Keep him there until you sell to him. Find out *why* he turned his back on you. So you ask yourself: "At what point in my presentation did that prospect lose interest? What went haywire? *Why* did I lose him? Did I let down on my appeal to his self-interest? Did I fail to notice a faint flicker of interest and ignore it? Did I cut in on him and talk myself out of a sale? You now see it all in a new light. You see how that prospect can be sold. You call on him again. You begin at the beginning. You show him how his best interests can be served by buying what you have to sell. You keep him and his welfare in the spotlight. You sell him what you should have sold him on the first call.

The successful specialty salesman whom we previously discussed found the answer to his two big questions. Some of his prospects froze on him. By self-examination he found out what to do with them. He rediscovered the magic warmth in *Secrets of the Hard Sell.* By self-discipline that salesman stepped out of the $5,000 bracket and up into the $25,000 class, and he continued to climb.

When a prospect freezes on us, our pride may be pricked. We may forget that humility often is an asset in selling. At one time Dwight L. Moody warned his readers about humility. "Be humble," he said, "or you'll stumble." Salesmen might well bear that in mind. Many of us talk our way out of sales. The novice is most apt to do this. However, humility has upgraded many novice salesmen into the "pro" class. Their humility, their sincerity served as a magnet. This is the REFINED HARD SELL. It recognizes the importance of the other fellow. Ralph Waldo Emerson had this slant on humility, which can be profitable to all sales people: "Every man I meet is my superior in some way. In that, I learn of him."

A veteran salesman once suggested to me that "nothing is impossible in selling." He then added: "Right now is the best time to tackle the prospect who yesterday turned you down."

That seasoned salesman, whom prospects had snubbed, maintained that there are just three classes of salesmen: (a) The beginner; (b) the self-satisfied; (c) the "pro." He may have been right. Today's case records reveal that the big sales are closed by "big" men with "big" aspirations and "big" salable ideas. Regardless of the category into which these "big" salesmen fall, they are motivated by the following three-point formula for landing "big" accounts:

1. WISE HEADWORK.
2. THOUGHTFUL MOUTH WORK.
3. TIRELESS FOOT WORK.

Those salesmen have crushed doubts. You and I can also do this. They have moved boldly into action. This, too, you and I can do.

Regardless of barriers encountered, those salesmen remain strong in heart. When the wind is against them, they adjust their sails and go after sales. They believe in themselves. They believe in what they have to sell. They believe in the magic power in *Secrets of the Hard Sell.*

Counter an Insult with Hard Sell Diversion
to Stimulate Buying Action

Many baby-sitters have found the SECRET of diversion to counter difficult situations. Salesmen might well observe babysitters in action.

Baby-sitters have mastered the "sweetening" art. They profit by it. They tempt upset babies and tame them. An efficient baby-sitter changes the thought direction of a screaming baby. This we call diversion.

When your prospects rant and thump their desks, what do you do? You should do as the baby-sitter does. You should act. You should do something. You could take a tip from the baby-sitter you observed. "How sweet it is" when the baby calms down. "How sweet it is" when a salesman counters a prospect's insolent showmanship with his own HARD SELL SHOWMANSHIP.

When a cantankerous prospect attempts to turn you off, he may divert you from your course. But you called on that prospect to sell. You believed you could sell your product to him. You believed your product would benefit him in some way. When you made your proposal, he blew up. Now, if you allow that rebuff to stop you in your tracks, then you lose. Equally important, your prospect gains nothing. At this point you have an alternative. You can counter with HARD SELL DIVERSION. You can act to swing his thinking into another channel. What could be more tantalizing to your obstinate prospect than a tempting idea? You could tempt him with prospects of greater profits? Or more comfort in living. You could tempt him with a proposal showing that your product can add "sweetness" to his life.

In difficult situations, take a tip from H. F. Amiel, a Swiss professor who declared: "He who does not advance falls back. The stationary condition is the beginning of the end." What an inspiring thought that is for us who sell. When a prospect is in a grumbling mood, we need action to solve that problem. When your prospect shows his teeth, toss him a "sweetener." Or do anything positive that is appealing. Your prospect, in his sour mood, needs to be "sweetened," even with a HARD SELL sweetener. Move ahead!

HARD SELL DIVERSION is practiced every day, even by children. For example, a girl came to my door at a busy moment. She was selling cookies for a worthy cause. But, she had interrupted me in a crisis. I was gruff. I told her I was too busy. I had the door almost closed when that girl turned on her HARD SELL CHARM. She offered me a cookie. "Taste it," she said. There was excitement in her voice and in her eyes. I could almost hear her thoughts—"Taste that cookie and you'll buy all right." Her smile added to her HARD SELL MAGIC. "They're very good cookies," she persisted. "Just taste one." That did the trick. I tasted and I bought.

That little girl demonstrated that persistence pays. She demonstrated that gruffness, near insolence, and other objectionable rebuffs in selling can be effectively countered by persistence and a "sweetener." That girl showed me how to counter a turndown by diversion. She used a "sweetener," a cookie, to divert my thoughts from not buying to tasting. She persisted and I succumbed to her HARD SELL MAGIC.

Principle: In your selling, counter insults (or any other form of refusal to buy) with HARD SELL DIVERSION. Stimulate thoughts of buying. Get action.

Dollar-Power Tips for Rewarming the Prospect's Buying Interest

Dollar-power tips include sales-producing HARD SELL FACTS. No tips, no amount of talk outsell solid, indisputable facts. Your most impressive sales demonstrations are those which capitalize on facts. The appeal is in facts about you, about your firm, and about what you have for sale.

When a prospect "freezes" rewarm his buying interest with facts. It's the sure-fire, HARD SELL technique.

The fact list which follows deals with many facts. Check this list. It can add dollar power to your selling. Add to this list all the tips that must have come your way. Check all tips for facts. Add to this list those facts which you know have produced sales for other salesmen.

Make fact-finding an obsession. Become a "know-it-all" salesman. Also become a "want to know it all" salesman. Become a reliable source of dollar-power information for your prospects.

Here, then, is your initial list of DOLLAR-POWER FACTS:

DOLLAR-POWER FACTS ABOUT OTHERS.—Exploit facts about other people. Show how they have benefited by using or reselling your product. Name those who have benefited. Your prospect may know them. This adds dollar power to your dollar-fact presentation.

DOLLAR-POWER FACTS FROM OTHERS.—Testimonials have HARD SELL power. When users testify that your product is great they are handing dollar power to you. Written recommendations of your product have dollar power. Written recommendations of you or of your firm provide you with a dollar-power label of dependability.

DOLLAR-POWER FACTS ABOUT THE MARKET.— Records of consumer demand have dollar power for you as a salesman. Through such reports you can inform your prospect of how he can profit by stocking or using your product.

DOLLAR-POWER FACTS ABOUT PRESTIGE.—Your prospect prefers to be identified with the top echelon in the community. Tell him and show him how and why he can gain prestige by handling or using your product. Give him facts. Present records to show that men and women of status are enthusiastic about your product. Explain why this is so. Let facts glorify your product and the brand name. Prestige-building facts have dollar power in them for you.

DOLLAR-POWER FACTS ABOUT DURABILITY.—Produce factual records to prove your claims of durability. This is a more-for-the-money point. It has HARD SELL power. Let facts stress the dollar value in long service.

DOLLAR-POWER FACTS ABOUT SEASONS.—If your product has year-around popularity capitalize on this point. It has dollar power. Hammer away on month-after-month high sales records for your product. Magnify the enjoyment of season-after-season usage of your product.

DOLLAR-POWER FACTS ABOUT TURNOVER.—This has its own dollar power. Turnover is a winner in the retail market. When your product has a record of fast movement it's a winner. Capitalize on this dollar-making power.

DOLLAR-POWER FACTS ABOUT QUALITY.—Brag about the quality of your product. Then prove it with facts. Make it believable. Show why it is superior. Proven quality claims have HARD SELL dollar-power.

DOLLAR-POWER FACTS ABOUT YOU.—The "me" approach can have dollar-power in selling. Show your prospect how your qualifications can mean dollar-power for him. Sell your prospect on you. Sell him on your product. Link the two with HARD SELL facts.

DOLLAR-POWER FACTS ABOUT HIM.—The more you know about your prospect the greater your HARD SELL power. Relate the dollar-power of your product to your prospect and to his plans. Convince your prospect that he has the special dollar power that fits his requirements.

HARD SELL FACTS ABOUT BENEFITS.—Become a benefactor. Load your sales presentations with facts about benefits for your prospect. Show how these benefits are enlarged upon by the quality of your product and the service of your firm. Show him! Tell him! Convince him! Sell him! Those are four dollar-power thrusts in the *Secrets of the Hard Sell.*

DOLLAR-POWER FACTS ABOUT TIME.—Fleeting minutes have great dollar power. If your product or service can save time for your prospect, it has dollar-making power. Tell your prospect about it. Show him how it can be done. Show him how much this time-saving feature means to him. He'll listen. And, by the magic power in the *Secrets of the Hard Sell* you can inspire him to buy.

DOLLAR-POWER FACTS ABOUT SECRETS OF THE HARD SELL.—In any product or service on the market you can find one or more features that can be exploited better with *Secrets of the Hard Sell.* Those SECRETS can lift you above the crowd in salesmanship. They have proven dollar power in selling. They have proven dollar power for rewarming "frozen" prospects. Capitalize on the magic power in HARD SELL FACTS.

How to Swing the Prospect Around to Your Viewpoint with the Magic Power in Secrets of the Hard Sell

The prospect we have in mind had scored millions in the construction business. He had been eyed by an insurance agent. He, too, had made the million-dollar club in his field. I saw that salesman leave the office of his prime prospect. A few minutes later I entered. I quipped to that construction genius: "I'd almost dare to bet that he sold you a neat package of insurance." My friend's eyebrows flicked. "Nobody, but nobody can sell me anything," he chuckled. "I buy what I want and that's that." He let the cat out of the bag when he added this: "One thing about that insurance fellow: I like him. The more he talked to me, the more I realized that it might be good business for me to increase my coverage a few thousand. I told him to drop in tomorrow and I'd have him fix me up with what I wanted. That's the way I do business. Nobody sells me anything. I just buy a lot, when it pays me to buy."

My estimate of that insurance salesman went up. Obviously, he had a firm grasp on the SECRET of swinging a hard-to-sell prospect around to his viewpoint. In his interviews with that prospect he had been releasing the magic power in *Secrets of the Hard Sell*. He had been making it easy for that self-sufficient prospect to have his own way. He had been making it so easy for that prospect to buy.

The skilled horseman does much the same thing in handling a high-spirited animal. He gives the horse his head. He allows the animal a certain freedom. Yet, he holds on to the reins. So it was with that HARD SELL insurance agent. He was dealing with a high-spirited prospect. He profited by giving him his head and holding on to the reins until he had made the sale.

There is an old idea, also, that you can lead a horse to water but you can't make him drink. So it often is with a tough prospect. One SECRET OF THE HARD SELL is to lead your prospect to the point of closing and then let him have his head. Give him enough freedom to act much as the horse acted. He'll "drink" when he gets good and ready to do so. The prospect who "never had been sold anything" was on the brink of buying. He was about to drink of the water to which he had been led. The salesman had "unbridled" him. This gave him a feeling of freedom. So, in his due time, he "just decided to buy that insurance." He never did concede that he had been sold.

The art of bringing our prospects around to our viewpoints is not complicated. It is simply this: Make it easy for them to buy. Tempt them. Make your products or your services appear to be very desirable. Be patient, but persistent. Most people are willing to be led. Stubborn prospects balk when they feel that they are being shoved.

Communication is the SECRET of many sales successes. This SECRET contains the magic of getting along with people. "Know your prospects well," was the motto of one top producer on my list. He seldom shoved. He pushed with firm gentleness. He invited pleasant, agreeable responses. He had mastered the art of exerting pressure gently but effectively. This had magic power. It is a SECRET OF THE HARD SELL.

Some time ago, I examined some of my own records of closed sales. They were illuminating. I classified them. I separated "good" from the "bad" days. I tried to find the answer to why some days were "good" and some "bad." Here is the result of my self-evaluation:

1. Business was good when I had been able to swing my prospects around to my viewpoint. My study convinced me that this had been accomplished by the magic power in *Secrets of The Hard Sell.*

2. Business was "spotty" on those days when I had not given time and thought to building and maintaining my lines of communication. I saw where I had neglected to get on a first name basis with prospects. I saw that I had not developed that sure, confident attitude in prospects which makes them customers.

3. Planned days were among my top producers. Haphazard days were on the "bad" list. Planned days had conserved my time and my energy. Planned days seemed to have given me reserve power for closing tough accounts. I lacked enthusiasm on the haphazard

days. The record clearly indicated that my prospects were not enthusiastic either on those days. It appeared that I had just been making calls. Not really selling.

4. My self-study showed up long days as top producers. My best days began at 8 a.m. and closed when the business in sight was wrapped up. At times, challenging calls were planned for evening.

5. Attitude was a winner in my self-evaluation. Most sales I closed were those I had believed I could close. Those were the accounts I had approached with an attitude of challenge. Sure victory had been clearly in my mind.

6. Clarity had magic power in my self-evaluation. The record was plain. Sales had come easier when I hit prospects with a concrete idea. Vague proposals fell flat. Prospects of benefits for prospects had selling power. My promises had been believable. I had backed them up with proof of fulfillment. My promises had been sound. Not fairy tales.

Keys that have opened doors for me to sales successes have been given to me by a number of my colleagues. These men have proved themselves to be masters in the art of employing *Secrets of the Hard Sell*. Among these keys are the following:

SERVE AND SELL.—Seize every opportunity to serve your prospects and customers. Strike to make service the basis of every sale.

YOUR TIME AND MY TIME.—Be considerate of your prospect's time. Conserve your own.

HERE'S YOUR HAT.—If your prospect shows signs of boredom or preoccupation, get out. Wait for better selling climate.

CASH IN ON FAILURES.—Put every failure through your personal laboratory. There must be a reason why a sale was lost. Find that reason. Profit by it.

BAITED TRAPS.—The bait to argue is often a trap for salesmen. Arguments seldom lead to sales. Some provocative prospects are specialists in baiting salesmen. Don't nibble. Instead, outsell them.

INFLATE 'EM AND SELL 'EM.—Sincerely praise prospects and customers whenever an opportunity arises. Sincere praise is a winner. But, don't be a flannel-mouth. Insincerity is quickly detected.

A young investment salesman was jubilant when he came into my office. He had landed his first substantial sale. "How did you do it?" I asked. Even before calling on me he had written down what he believed to be his winning points in landing that sale. These were his notes:

> (a) I caught his interest early. I gave him facts to show that his investment would be safe with us . . . that his return would be good. When he questioned me on this point, I kept at it in every direction and in every interview. Finally, I closed the sale on security and earnings.
>
> (b) Before I could talk security to him, I had to gain his confidence. While doing this I was also selling him on the firm I represented.
>
> (c) Free communication was my first objective. This proved to be the vital step in closing the sale. When we got on friendly, business-like speaking terms, the rest went smoothly.

It is significant to note that both the insurance salesman and the investment salesman anchored their sales to the solid rock of communication. Then, through *Secrets of the Hard Sell,* both of those salesmen were able to swing their prospects around to their viewpoints.

How to Crush Insults by Inviting Commitments on Self-Interest Ideas

There was a time when an insult was a challenge. Personal honor was at stake. A duel was the only solution. In today's fast-action world of selling, an insult has another flavor. An insult may be a "stopper." If it does stop the salesman, he is a loser. He came there to sell. An insult is an obstacle that HARD SELL salesmen take in stride. A duel would get the salesman nowhere. But the magic power in *Secrets of the Hard Sell* usually produces sales, even in the face of insults. Case records show that insults often pave the way to closed sales.

When your next prospect flies off the handle, pick up the challenge. Your course lies in quick-thinking and BOLD SELLING.

Ignore your prospect's insults. Never let him get you on the defensive.

When your prospect has released his venom, tempt him. Drop a casual hint that he has been overlooking an opportunity for profit. Before he tears that suggestion apart, fire another self-interest shot at him. For instance, you might tell him about a colleague of his who has unloaded a carload of mattresses in a smashing 12-hour sale. Or you might tip him off that another progressive merchant is creating a special showroom to bid for brides' business.

It really doesn't matter what business your prospect is in, you have cooled his negative attitude. You have got him thinking about others who are building instead of growling. Counter suggestions are thought-starters. They are diversionary shots. They tend to get your insolent prospect into calmer waters. He becomes easier to sell.

The double-barreled SECRET of cooling an insolent prospect is this: (1) Counter action; (2) self-interest action. This deflates an insolent prospect. He suddenly becomes aware of losing money while he is spewing venom on a salesman. The SECRET is to delay his attack. Slow him down just long enough to commit himself on an idea. One commitment on a good idea will let out his steam.

A jewelry salesman, whom I'll identify as Tom Wesley, was known as a "cooler." An insolent prospect was his dish. A cantankerous prospect intrigued him. Insults flew past that salesman's consciousness like feathers on the wind. An angry thrust bounced off and left no bruises on him. He said: "I never allow a dirty crack to leave a mark on me. I just let such prospects boil. I wait for an opener to toss in a cooler. Generally, such prospects work themselves out of their own stew. They get no kick out of talking to a guy who won't respond. When one of those has unwound, I go in to sell. It usually works. This is understandable. When a prospect realizes he is gasping for breath and getting nowhere, he is willing to be shown. He's ready to be sold."

Tom's SECRET seems to have a tie-in with this bit of wisdom from the best-selling book of all time: "If thine enemy be hungry, give him bread to eat; and if he be thirsty, give him water to drink." (Prov. 25:21)

You may ask: "Why not avoid the offensive prospects?" The answer is: They will buy from someone. Why not from you? Thomas Carlyle put it this way: "No man lives without jostling and being jostled; in all ways he has to elbow himself through the world, giving and receiving offense."

A successful securities salesman I know maintains that self-interest often is the very thing that overwhelms a difficult prospect. Leonard Reed, president of The Foundation for Economic Education, Inc., states: "Everything is self-interest oriented, and, in this we are all alike. As regards self-interest we differ only in our interpretation of how it is best served."

The Principle: Cool your belligerent prospect with self-interest ideas. Let him in on the SECRET. Tell him how he can profit. Suggest how he can make an easy buck. Press him for favorable commitments on constructive ideas. When he nods once, you are on your way. When he says "yes" you have quenched the flame. His thoughts have been diverted from telling you off to gaining something for himself. Basically this is a big SECRET OF THE HARD SELL.

How to Cool Insolence with Friendly Warmth Plus Full Power of Hard Sell Magic

Motives of unpleasant prospects are fascinating. By simply exploring these motives we gain insight into new fields of opportunities for selling.

Insolent prospects may not be as vicious as we might expect. In many cases they are fishing for information. They may be testing our ability to cope with an unpleasant situation. They may even be open to proposals that promise benefits for them. In other words they haven't shut out the possibility that we might hold the key to benefits they desire to gain. All of this presents a formidable challenge to any salesman. With this in mind, let us examine a typical run of prospects which you and I may meet almost any day:

DIFFICULT PROSPECTS	TRACTABLE PROSPECTS
Insolent	Affable
Quarrelsome	Neighborly
Argumentative	Cordial
Distant	Genial
Indifferent	Sociable

Self-examination is now in order. We, too, can be classified. We are either negative or positive. This shows up in our daily sales records:

NEGATIVE SALESMEN	POSITIVE SALESMEN
Pessimistic	Optimistic
Reluctant	Persuasive
Contrary	Enthusiastic
Cock-sure	Convincing
Rebellious	Resourceful
Aloof	Friendly

Top salesmen identify with the positive group. They are aggressive men. Unpleasant prospects challenge them. They keep their objective in mind under all circumstances—TO SELL. They persist in getting through to growling, insolent, unpleasant prospects. They summon all they know about winning friends and influencing people. They may not have learned this directly from Dale Carnegie. However, the techniques involved have rubbed off on them as they made their way through various market places. Business has long recognized that friendship comes through the smoke of battle with a dollar sign on it. Great industries spend millions in "public relations" programs. This is a fancy name for old-fashioned, down-to-earth friendship. The latter has warmth.

Eventually it can thaw out the frozen resistance of the most unpleasant prospects. Elbert Hubbard once defined a friend as: "One who knows all about you and loves you the same." Salesmen who take that to heart build sales volume. They profit by friendship. The sincere ones rise to great heights. The insincere fall by the wayside. The struggle for favor in the market place is rugged.

A salesman for a large paper products concern corraled the choicest accounts in his territory. He served them well. His accounts believed in him. I asked one of his largest customers why that salesman was so successful. The customer replied: "He makes friends and he keeps them." This bears out what J. C. Penney once said: "Success in life does not depend on genius."

The paper products salesman merchandised friendship. He made no fuss about his good deeds. It was just natural for him to act that way. This was his great asset. Broken down, this is a pattern of his operation:

(a) He found ways to do something to benefit or to please obstinate people. He made friends by being a friend. He was helpful to the most cantankerous prospects he encountered.

(b) When sales situations became rowdy, he remained calm. When sales resistance became tough, he held to the pleasant line. He never backed up. He constantly gained ground. Inch by inch. He exchanged smiles for frowns. Maintaining this friendly bearing, he gained in influence. He led. Insolent prospects fell in line behind him. He was resourceful.

A syndicate salesman topped the field in sales. His product was the output of gifted writers and cartoonists. He was a moneymaker for himself. The syndicate he represented profited by his HARD SELL SUCCESS SECRETS. His sales brought to the writers and cartoonists the pleasure and satisfaction of substantial royalties. This salesman was a friendly gentleman. He put me in mind of what Ralph Waldo Emerson once wrote: "A friend is someone who will make us do what we can when we are saying we can't."

It took a hard-nosed editor to cause that syndicate salesman to pause one day. But the salesman soon got the inspiration to score another victory for himself. Sarcastically the editor said: "I could drop what we are using of your line and I doubt that many readers would miss the stuff." After a long and thoughtful eye-to-eye contact with his editor-prospect that salesman replied: "I always had high regard for your editorial judgment. I still do. You've been buying features from me for about ten years. Each year, when you renew or revise your contract, my estimate of you goes up a notch. I notice, too, that your circulation continues to climb. This is a tribute to your sound editorial judgment. Now, here's a new contract. It's a renewal with two new features added. I have written both of them in. This gives you first crack at them and exclusive rights for publication in your circulation territory." He handed a pen to the cigar-chewing editor. He signed. How did that salesman put it over? By BOLD SELLING. He had the following six points in his favor all the time:

1. HE KNEW HIS LINE WELL.
2. HE KNEW THE TEMPER OF THE ONE HE WAS SERVING.
3. HE KNEW THE POSSIBILITIES FOR THOSE HE PLANNED TO SERVE.
4. HE WORKED HARD. HE PLANNED AHEAD.
5. HE WAS ENTHUSIASTIC, OPTIMISTIC, SELF-CONFIDENT.
6. HE WON FRIENDS. HE KEPT THEM.

Principle: Recognize that a prospect's insolence often is evidence of weakness. Strengthen those insolent prospects. Extend to them a hand of friendship. Turn on the warmth of firm, HARD SELL friendship. Help them build their own self-confidence. Insolence may be a temporary sales obstacle. Usually it crumbles under the magic power in *Secrets of the Hard Sell.*

12

Regaining Lost Business Through Hard Sell Magic

At times, salesmen are haunted men. They are haunted by ghosts of lost sales. The mystery of why a solid account goes sour haunts them. Faced with such nagging problems, the salesman must do one of two things: Either he must resell that lost account, or he must replace that lost account with new business. On the surface this seems to be quite simple. Nevertheless, it can become a haunting problem.

I have known seasoned salesmen who attacked this ghost with HARD SELL LOGIC. They rolled up their sleeves and shooed away those haunting things by bold selling. They turned on the magic power in *Secrets of the Hard Sell*.

Most salesmen in virtually all lines are vulnerable to the jolt of lost business. They build accounts to substantial size. Then those accounts become targets for competing salesmen. To condition himself to cope with such eventualities, one HARD SELL salesman I observed disciplined himself. He kicked out the lost sale ghost that tried to haunt him. This one question nagged him into action: Why did I lose those accounts? So he broke down his lost sales into categories. This is what he came up with:

1. "NO EXCUSE" LOST SALES. (He assured himself that he could beat that problem. He reasoned that a

prospect who quits with no reason or excuse should not be too hard to sell or resell.)

2. PRACTICALLY CLOSED SALES THAT WENT SOUR. (Those losses required a rerun of the whole selling drama. He found a way to get them back. He "sweetened" them as he had in the beginning. He released upon them the magic power of the HARD SELL.)

3. SALES LOST BY ARGUMENT. (He soon discovered that arguments do not close sales. Arguments create sales barriers.)

4. THE "BETTER DEAL" LOSSES. (He subdued this form of resistance by factual presentations. By BOLD SELLING. By the magic in HARD SELL FACTS.)

5. THE "SECURE" ACCOUNTS THAT QUIT. (These were the real mystery accounts. They taught him this lesson: "All accounts need to be resold on each call." Unless we do this, we become order-takers.)

HARD SELL MAGIC saved accounts for that salesman in each of the foregoing categories. Records of many beginning salesmen provide proof of similar results. Records of salesmen who have won their stripes by long service demonstrate that *Secrets of the Hard Sell* really can recover lost accounts.

HARD SELL MAGIC has strong recovery power. With a combination of BOLD SELLING plus the magic power in the HARD SELL and in *Secrets of the Hard Sell,* lost sales are being recovered. Losses are also being cut down by the same magic power.

—SECRET OF SELLING TO THE NO-EXCUSE QUITTER:—Hammer away on him with fresh ideas of how he can enjoy more personal benefits by buying what you have to sell. Reactivate his desire to have, to buy.

—SECRET OF OUTSELLING THE "PRACTICALLY SOLD" SYNDROME:—No sale is closed until it is closed. An overnight wait can be fatal. A mystery character may slip into the picture during the night.

Principle: Close while the prospect is warm. "Strike while the iron is hot."

—SECRET OF RECOVERING SALES LOST IN ARGU- MENTS:—Make a quick, sincere apology. This does two things: (a) It feeds the ego of your prospect. It emphasizes his importance. (b) It clears the atmosphere for orderly closing of a sale.

—SECRET OF OUTSELLING THE "BETTER DEAL" OBSTACLE:—Concentrate on cold, hard facts. Itemize points at issue, point by point. Compare. If your prospect seems to have a better deal in some respect agree with him. Then build up the benefits you can offer in quality, in style, in comfort, in service, in all over dependability of what you have for sale. Hammer hard on endurance. Hammer hard on the known reputation of the firm you represent. Hammer hard on known quality, and the no-risk feature. Sell him on this idea: "Actually, what I am offering you costs a little more, but it's worth more. Surely you deserve the best for your money."

—SECRET OF RESELLING THE LONG ESTABLISHED ACCOUNT WHO QUITS:—Dig deep for the real reason of this prospect's dissatisfaction. Sidestep any attempt to draw you into argument. Grant that your prospect must have a valid reason for his disenchantment. Find that reason. The real reason. It may just be that you have been taking that prospect too much for granted. It may be that he feels that with so much business tossed to you he deserves just a little more personal attention than he has been getting. Have you been taking that solid, old account too much for granted? If so begin now to woo him again. Selling is a con- stant thing. Never let up.

Solving the Mystery of Why Customers Break Away and Hard Sell Secrets of Getting Them back

Your most productive field for new business right now might well be your drop-out customers.

You may have given too little time to those once loyal customers since they broke away from you.

You may have guessed why they chose to buy elsewhere. But, did you really find out why?

You may have assumed a "so-what" attitude toward them.

You may have been reluctant to dig into their problems.

You may have never solved the real mystery of the break-off.

Time may now have caused you to take another look at that rich area you have left untouched. You may have begun to review the losses you have sustained by those dropouts. You may also have let your pencil scratch out a few figures on the possibilities which still lie in the hands of those former accounts. With this you may now be gazing out in their direction with your own self-interest in mind. It's now in your interest to solve the break-away mystery. Through *Secrets of the Hard Sell* you can get them back on your books. It's being done every day.

Burt Alderman is a food products salesman. He told me how he solved the mystery of a lost customer. He discovered that he was the one at fault. He had been satisfied to supply the "needs" as the stockman declared those needs to be. He now sees that he had really not been selling. He had tried to convince himself that his line showed up well on the customer's shelves. He reasoned that the shelf display was proof enough of his own good work. But now it is clear to him that he had been negligent in other directions. For instance, he had ignored the steady growth of competing lines on his customer's shelves. Stockmen with whom he had long been on first-name speaking terms explained that "the boss" was excited about the new lines. They washed their hands of responsibility. "We haven't any control over that," they assured their friendly salesman. That, of course, reminded Burt that he had never really acquainted himself with the manager's objectives and his problems. It is clear to him now that he hadn't really been doing any HARD SELLING. He had been taking orders from the stockman. That was easy-come business. He liked it. But, then it faded away. This cleared up the mystery. He turned to BOLD SELLING. His volume began to rise. It's high now. He's progressing in high gear, thanks to *Secrets of the Hard Sell*.

Something similar to this happened to an automotive supply salesman. The shop foreman had been his main contact. He had done little selling beyond that point. What he was getting he called "nice business." But, then, one day the foreman told him that some changes had been made. He had received orders from the higher echelon of executives to take on a competing line of supplies. This salesman, too, had failed to sell beyond the shop foreman. He was unknown to the higher echelon of executives. No personal contact had been developed there. He was late in unraveling the mystery of why his "solid" account broke away. By aggressive, bold reselling from the top down, that salesman eventually recovered that account.

The SECRET of recovering lost accounts is this:

(a) Find out all you can about your customer's business operation. Find out who is in command. Find out who has authority to buy in quantity. Search for ways to serve them.

(b) Learn all you can about the policy of your cusmer's business. Determine how your line fits into that policy. Then capitalize on it with bold selling, with *Secrets of the Hard Sell.*

(c) Establish communication with everyone who has an interest in or authority in buying. This provides you with a road map for BOLD SELLING. Get on speaking terms with as many members of the corporate family as you can. If an order comes to you through a subordinate, boost that subordinate's stock, to him and to those above him.

A direct salesman, selling house-to-house, forestalled many losses by a simple HARD SELL approach. The lady at the door had been one of his regular customers. She cut him off sharply. He suggested that "Mrs. Brown" had tried out his new cleaning compound, and she now claims that it is her biggest work-saver. Saving work interested the lady. In that moment, the would-be dropout became a live prospect again. The salesman proceeded from that point and turned a near dropout into an enthusiastic customer using many of his products.

An office supply salesman forestalled loss of an account by leaving samples of a new ribbon development with every secretary and typist in the office. He captured the interest and favor of these working people. He then went in to those who had the authority to buy in quantity. He told them he had left samples with their staff. This interested them. They would be asking those secretaries about that new ribbon. He advised those executives that he would come back and recheck results with the staff. He also assured the executives that he would report to them the results of his recheck. This further interested them. It indicated to them that this salesman had their welfare in mind. He was more than an order-taker. This was BOLD SELLING. He created confidence. This attitude opened doors for him. This is another SECRET OF THE HARD SELL.

Coleman duPont once told his colleagues in business: "There are certain fundamental principles which, once mastered, can be utilized in almost any line of business." One principle which directly applies to salesmen is this: "The greatest piece of information in the world will do you no good if you do not respond to it."

Principle: Every salesman should be an investigator. Know your product. Know its uses. Know your prospects and your customers. Know their needs. Neglect of customers encourages dropouts. Service to customers discourages drop-outs. The HARD SELL SECRET of getting dropout customers back is to glorify them. Maintain solid lines of communication with them.

Magic Lure of Profit to Halt Business from Skipping Away

A creative, far-seeing, radio-time advertising salesman halted a skidding account by flashing dollar-making ideas at his customer. He resold an entire spot advertising program in that way to a supermarket chain.

For some time, that salesman had suspected that his account was cooling off on the contract. He became uneasy. To forestall loss of the contract, he persuaded the advertising director to have his accounting department dig out an over-all month-by-month gain or loss in volume since they had launched the current spot campaign. The advertising director jumped at the idea. To his amazement, and also that of the salesman, each market in the chain showed a volume increase since the spot campaign had been launched.

As the salesman told me: "It was possible that something else was involved in all that increase. Other factors than the spot advertising campaign might have been the cause. But, you can bet your money, I tied that increase tight to those radio spots. In my resale pitch, I tied that volume increase to the advertising director's wisdom in charting the course of the campaign. I provided him with a HARD SELL package to carry up to his superiors. Up there it is often a case of 'how much will it cost,' rather than 'what can we realistically expect from this venture.' Usually those people are not gamblers. They deal in profit realities. So, the figures we had obtained showed heavy increases during the progress of the advertising campaign. Those increases were timed with spot schedule. Using those figures of dollar increases, I dangled the magic lure of profit before them. I tied those profits to radio spots on my station. As a result, I put the brakes on a skidding contract which I am sure I would have lost. My personal income would have taken a beating. The broadcasting firm I represent would have suffered a loss. And, naturally, I must also believe that my customer would have lost if the contract had been dropped. Didn't the accountant's figures prove that? At least, they were convincing enough to save the account."

This was BOLD SELLING. In case after case, the HARD SELL line turns out to be the profit line. The profit line works to get new business. It does its share in halting established business from slipping out of the salesman's fingers.

If our minds are receptive, we learn from each HARD SELL experience. An account gone sour challenges us. We strike back. We try to pump renewed solidity into the account.

In this action we may discover that we, too, need a shot in the arm. It dawns on us that the magic lure of profit has dazzling brilliance on both sides of the coin. (1) The profit line spurs relaxed salesmen on to new and higher goals. (2) The profit line spurs your prospect to listen intently. You then unfold for him new ideas for money-making. If you have done your work well, you will sell!

This constant learning from victory to disappointment, and

from disappointment to victory, has a profit side for salesmen. This point moved Coleman duPont to declare: "Constant learning prevents stagnation, and insures both financial and mental growth."

Salesmen draw their greatest power in creating something that profits somebody. Note these steps: (a) They get an idea. (b) They expand that idea. (c) They give that idea life and growth. (d) They continue to toy with that idea. (e) Finally, that idea takes form.

That idea now has become something tangible. Soon it will be throwing its weight around. It may become a potent force in that salesman's efforts. Or it may become a potent force in his customer's business. When it does, it has created money power. It has become a profitable idea. That idea may even result in greater profits. That idea may create new business. That idea may result in greater profits to many buyers. It may also mean greater profits to other salesmen.

An idea of merit is destined to become a magnetic force. It can hold customers close to you. It can also halt business from slipping away from you.

The magic lure of profit builds homes. It builds business establishments. It creates great industries. It drives salesmen on and on to stimulate sales.

The magic lure of profit also has HARD SELL power. If there's an extra buck to be made, the most uneasy prospect settles down and buys. The big SECRET OF THE HARD SELL is to exalt the profit motive. In the minds of prospective buyers the profit motive has endless possibilities. Sales that total five or six figures, and even more, are closed because somebody involved had the vision to detect the profit possibilities in the deal.

At some point in the negotiations which closed some of the largest sales on record the *Secrets of the Hard Sell* became involved.

Secret Value of a Fresh Image in Recapturing Lost Business

Even a schoolboy knows the value of a fresh image. When he senses that he has lost prestige with his teacher, he goes the extra mile. He musters new courage. He stirs up new enthusiasm for recapturing what he has lost. He washes his face. He decides that a fresh image will get him back in the favored groove.

In taking this face-washing step, the schoolboy aims at impressing his teacher. He is doing more than presenting a cleanly washed face. He is presenting a fresh image. He believes that a fresh image will have magic power in recapturing lost favor. To salesmen that schoolboy's point of view is understandable. What he did was this: He called upon the magic power in *Secrets of the Hard Sell* to get him back in the groove in school. In a few years it may be clear to him that he succeeded by BOLD SELLING.

Image-making is becoming a fine art in salesmanship. Check the following SECRETS of recapturing lost business. They have proved their magic power in presenting a fresh image to prospects:

1. SECRET OF CHANGING ATTITUDE to present a fresh image.

2. SECRET OF EMPLOYING SELF-DISCIPLINE to change your image.

3. SECRET OF CULTIVATING A FRESH IMAGE by changing one's attitude toward the job.

4. SECRET OF INCREASING HARD SELL POWER by improving our IMAGE.

"If you don't like a situation, change your attitude." This is the advice of Golden R. Driggs, a successful business executive. This could be the positive approach for recapturing lost business. Change your attitude and then go after recovering that lost business.

Another business executive declared that to become outstanding at anything, it's all a matter of attitude. Earl Nightingale, whose stature is well known to salesmen, has demonstrated the truth of this statement.

Your greatest challenge in selling may be to recapture lost business. It probably will require more BOLD SELLING than you displayed at the moment you lost the business.

Attitude has had dynamic power in driving salesmen to attain greatness. Success has become their compensation for changing their attitude. The point is this: *Change your attitude and you immediately change your image.*

Enthusiasm is contagious. It is an allied power in image-changing. Enthusiasm affects your prospect as it affects you. It generates favorable interest. It generates wholesome, productive excitement. Your enthusiastic prospect is seeing a situation as you, in your enthusiasm, have presented it. He becomes less argumentative. He approves more. He resists less. All this is happening because you changed your attitude. All this happened because you returned to him with a fresh attitude. You changed your image. You were all dressed up to recapture what you thought you had lost.

Change in attitude requires more than a flip of your fingers. It requires effort. It requires sincerity and the art of persuasion. A change in attitude has magic power. But there is little mystery about it. The sincere salesman capitalizes on it. This magic power surfaces at the right time through the force put behind it by the salesman with a HARD SELL power-thrust. All this is the product of self-discipline.

I met a friend who was walking at a faster pace than usual. He was a salesman. His attitude had changed. This was obvious. His step was firm. His voice had a positive tone. His chin was up. I asked: "Where are you headed?" He replied: "I'm going to resell an account that turned me down flat two days ago. I have decided I won't let that fellow get off the hook that easy. I've reworked my whole selling approach. I am determined to recapture that business." His plan was a winner. His change of image, his change of spirit, his change of attitude and a lot of self-discipline did the trick.

A fresh image can have magic power for you in selling. In case you get the cold shoulder from an account you figured on selling without a struggle, brace yourself. That fellow can be sold. Somebody will sell to him. The cold shoulder treatment was all due to a lower price made by a competitor; was that it? Here's a new-image idea that worked for an electrical appliance salesman. Instead of brooding over the loss, this salesman took himself in hand. This is the way he told it to me:

"I went back to that account before he could get around to buying another brand. I ducked the price angle. Instead, I went after him on investing in value. I got myself all worked up about the value of my product. Apparently my high spirit caught on with my prospect. It became apparent to me that I had succeeded in changing my image in his eyes. This, plus my change of attitude, resulted in changing my prospect's attitude. As I hammered away on value, he forgot about price. He began to ask about proof of endurance, quality, etc. My value pitch worked. He bought and my house joined him in a hot volume promotional project that upped my sales total for that month."

Principle: To recapture lost business do this:

(a) Reopen the mind of your prospect.
(b) INFLUENCE HIS THINKING INTO POSITIVE CHANNELS.
(c) Present a fresh, inspiring image.

All of the foregoing are SECRETS OF THE HARD SELL.

Hard Sell Two-for-One Magic in Recovering from Lost Business

This is the SECRET of two-for-one magic: *Replace a lost account with two new accounts.* Simple, isn't it?
How can we do this?
The answer lies in *Secrets of the Hard Sell.*
Few salesmen are selling as well as they know how. Had we been up to par with a decent batting average when we walked away from our last drop-out customer, chances are that we would have secured the business, not lost it. The plain fact is that our negative customer out-sold us.
Let's do a little more self-examination. Here are seven how-to-do-it tips. They are based on accomplishments of successful salesmen I have known. Take time out now to check them:

1. KEEP CONTACTING all former accounts. Never scratch them off your list of possibilities. Get those former accounts back into the fold. If you don't sell them, somebody else will.
2. KEEP UP creative selling with present and prospective accounts. This is your insurance against loss.

3. KEEP UP your enthusiasm. Draw your prospects into your excitement. Generate desire for your line and for your ideas.

4. CONCENTRATE on one BIG idea. Develop one BIG idea in each sales presentation. Avoid scatter-brain presentations.

5. SELL ASSOCIATE IDEAS. After the BIG one is closed add an "extra" to each order. It's amazing how those "extras" add up in volume.

6. ORGANIZE TO SELL MORE. Organize your time. Organize your presentations. Organize your follow-up schedules. Sell more per call by better organization. Get to your prospects easier and faster by organizing your routes for making calls.

7. KEEP RECORDS UP TO HARD SELL STANDARDS. Make records of customers and prospects complete and informative. Keep them up to date.

Here is your objective in two-for-one HARD SELL magic: To recover lost business and add a new account.

Alternate Objective: To open up two new accounts to replace the lost one.

Why?

Your two-for-one objective is to provide steady growth in number of accounts. To insure steady growth in total sales. To insure steady growth in your personal income.

I know many successful salesmen who rely on critical self-examination to learn why they have lost established accounts. The accounts they had lost were believed by them to have been secure. Then came the break. This was the shocker. Those accounts had been steady revenue producers. In case after case, those inquiring salesmen came up with these revealing answers to the mystery of lost business.

1. THEY HAD LET DOWN IN HARD SELL ENTHUSIASM. They had taken their steady customers for granted.

2. THEY HAD LET DOWN IN PREPARATION.
They had gone in too often with half-baked ideas.
They had gone after an order instead of doing HARD
SELL creative selling.

3. THEY HAD LET DOWN in clearly defining to
themselves why they were making each sales call.
They had surrendered to routine. They had neglected
creativity.

4. THEY HAD LET DOWN IN A WILL TO WIN.
As a result, sales resistance had taken over. Those
salesmen had lost their spirit. They had suffered shock
when the long established accounts broke their ties.
But, those lost accounts could be replaced. Those accounts should immediately go on the salesman's "live
prospect" list.

In all this, there is an element of mystery. When you go into
your own cases of lost accounts, the mystery makes each case an
intriguing story. Those successful salesmen I knew tried to solve
their mysteries. They began by prying into the No. 1 probability.
They took a HARD SELL look at their own performance. They
came up with two conclusions:

1. Lukewarm sales presentations lost business.
2. "Hot" sales presentations made sales. Bold selling has
miraculous qualities for regaining lost business.

The attitude of salesmen scored high in this survey of why they
had lost business. The successful salesmen came out of this inquiry
with top ratings in the following personal qualities:

1. They displayed quiet confidence in each presentation.
2. They maintained balance when under fire.
3. They met sales resistance head-on. They rose above
their obstacles.
4. They maintained a positive attitude.
5. They reflected a spirit of "I'll get this order." And,
they usually did. They sustained their enthusiasm,
even against losses. They maintained their self-con-

fidence. They took charge of each sales situation. They capitalized on *Secrets of the Hard Sell.* They influenced the thinking of their prospects.

Principle: Sales result from enthusiastic selling. Vigorous, colorful, factual presentations contain HARD SELL magic. Dropouts occur among salesmen as they do among established accounts.

How Multiple Hard Sell Power Reopens Doors to Replace Lost Accounts with Profitable Accounts

Constant prospecting is the SECRET of success in selling.

Normal attrition is said to draw off 20 percent of our accounts annually. This means that we must replace those accounts. We must also secure new accounts in anticipation of loss by attrition in the upcoming year. Obviously, we have but one alternative: To put more vigor into our search for desirable new prospects. The 20-percent approximation is only a "holding" figure. For a healthy gain we must make it more than a 20-percent gain in active accounts.

An automobile salesman I knew skipped up and out of the "average" classification. Selective prospecting made him a "star" salesman. By taking a cold look at his record, he found that he had been wasting time on unstable prospects. He had been working on prospects who had minimum need for a new car. Prospects who turned out to have low credit ratings had wasted his time. Prospects who were poor driving risks had high accident records. They were not the most desirable accounts to have on his list. By more selective prospecting, that salesman eliminated many time wasters. This enabled him to concentrate on "hot" prospects. He gained in status and in income by seeking out and selling to prospects of stability. In two years that salesman's income more than doubled. It continues to climb. Selective prospecting did this for him. He showed me his current list of buyers. Here's a glimpse at it:

1. CUSTOMERS WITH STABILITY.
2. CUSTOMERS WHO CAN BENEFIT by buying AUTOMOBILES.
3. CUSTOMERS WITH TOP CREDIT RATINGS
4. CUSTOMERS WITH CONSTRUCTIVE IDEAS for enjoying and profitably using automobiles.

5. CUSTOMERS OF STANDING who add prestige to the salesman's account list.

To achieve his objective, that automobile salesman did much the same as an insurance salesman I knew. Both turned to selective prospecting. They cut down the dropout rate among their customers. They added more new accounts than the total of their dropouts. By selective prospecting both of these salesmen enjoyed steadily increasing incomes.

Here are five HARD SELL qualifications that identify both the automobile salesman and the insurance salesman. These same qualifications might well be those of successful salesmen in almost any line on the market. There is no exclusiveness in HARD SELL requirements. For instance, note the sales-building power in the following five categories. You can apply any of these to your line, whatever that may be:

1. INITIATIVE.
2. INGENUITY.
3. RESOURCEFULNESS.
4. PERSISTENCE.
5. HARD SELL PERSUASIVE POWER.

But, it is MULTIPLE HARD SELL POWER that we seek to combat the dropout rate. This is the magic power that opens and reopens doors. It is this power that replaces lost accounts. It is this same power that draws new accounts to us. There are at least five points involved in this magic HARD SELL power. Note these:

1. DRAMATIZING THE ORDINARY by bold selling.
2. SUPPORTING CLAIMS by indisputable facts.
3. GLORIFYING ALL FEATURES that have self-interest appeal for prospects.
4. MAKING PRESENTATIONS REAL, COLORFUL, AND INCISIVE with hard sell word magic.
5. STIRRING UP BUYING FEVER for effective closing through the magic power in *Secrets of the Hard Sell.*

INDEX

199